Giving Thanks

Giving Thanks

Rediscovering the Heart of Gratitude

Philip Plyming

CANTERBURY
PRESS

© Philip Plyming 2025
First published in 2025 by the Canterbury Press Norwich

Editorial office
3rd Floor, Invicta House
110 Golden Lane,
London EC1Y 0TG, UK
www.canterburypress.co.uk

Canterbury Press is an imprint of Hymns Ancient & Modern Ltd
(a registered charity)

Hymns Ancient & Modern® is a registered trademark of
Hymns Ancient & Modern Ltd
13A Hellesdon Park Road, Norwich,
Norfolk NR6 5DR, UK

All rights reserved. No part of this publication may be reproduced,
stored in a retrieval system, or transmitted,
in any form or by any means, electronic, mechanical,
photocopying or otherwise, without the prior permission of
the publisher, Canterbury Press.

Philip Plyming has asserted his right under the Copyright, Designs and
Patents Act 1988 to be identified as the Author of this Work

Scripture quotations are from New Revised Standard Version Bible: Anglicized
Edition, copyright © 1989, 1995 National Council of the Churches of Christ in
the United States of America. Used by permission. All rights reserved worldwide.

British Library Cataloguing in Publication data
A catalogue record for this book is available
from the British Library

ISBN: 978-1-78622-643-3

EU GPSR Authorised Representative
LOGOS EUROPE, 9 rue Nicolas Poussin, 17000, LA ROCHELLE, France
E-mail: Contact@logoseurope.eu

No part of this book may be used or reproduced in any manner for the purpose
of training artificial intelligence technologies or systems.

Typeset by Regent Typesetting
Printed and bound in Great Britain by
CPI Group (UK) Ltd

To the community at Durham Cathedral

Contents

Acknowledgements	ix
Introduction – Let's Give Thanks	1

Part 1 – Getting Started: Foundations for a Thankful Life

1 A Pioneering Prayer: Introducing the General Thanksgiving	13
2 Who's on the Call? Seeing God and Ourselves Clearly	23
3 Everyday Thanks: Learning to Count Our Blessings	33

Part 2 – Love Beyond Measure: The Heart of Thankfulness

4 Love for the World: Christ's Gift of Redemption	45
5 Love for Today: The Means of Grace	55
6 Love Forever: The Hope of Glory	65

Part 3 – Living Gratefully: The Practice of a Thankful Life

7 Letting It Sink In: A Thankful Heart	77
8 Giving Up Ourselves: Leading Thankful Lives	87

9 It's Not About Us: All for the Glory of God   96

Conclusion – Praying the General Thanksgiving Today   105

Appendix – A Contemporary Form of the General Thanksgiving   114

Bibliography   115

Acknowledgements

Given the title of this book, it seems appropriate to start with some words of thanks.

This book has been written during my first two years serving as Dean of Durham, and I want to thank my staff colleagues and members of the worshipping community at the Cathedral who have welcomed me so warmly and helped me learn the ropes of an entirely new ministry. In particular I want to thank my colleagues Michael Hampel and Dan Parkinson for inducting me so generously into the patterns of cathedral worship, and encouraging me to use the General Thanksgiving as often as I liked in our services of Evensong. I was allowed to take some time away from normal duties to write this book, and I am grateful to Paul Chandler, Vice-Chair of Chapter, for encouraging me to do so, and to Guy Sampson, Chief Operating Officer at Durham Cathedral, for ensuring everything ran more smoothly in my absence.

The Prayer Book Society, of which I am a member, held their annual conference in Durham in 2024, and kindly invited me to give a keynote address on the General Thanksgiving. I am grateful to Bradley Smith for his invitation and to the conference participants for their appreciative engagement with my address. While it might be seen as preaching to the choir, their encouragement gave me hope that I had something useful to say on what has always been a favourite prayer of mine (and, it turns out, of many others as well).

David Hunt, Canon Emeritus at Durham Cathedral, and a regular at Choral Evensong, confessed to me his love of the General Thanksgiving, and found himself reading part of my work as a result. I am grateful for his doing so and his encouraging comments.

GIVING THANKS

Walter Moberly, my erstwhile teacher at Durham in the 1990s, continues to serve as my first reader and is a model of thoughtfulness and attentiveness in so doing. His marrying together of academic rigour and devotional heart is something I continue to find inspiring. Every comment he made gave me the chance to improve the final text; the errors and omissions that remain are, of course, my own.

I wrote this book knowing I was going to speak on the General Thanksgiving at an ordination retreat for curates from the Kensington area in the Diocese of London. I am grateful to Bishop Emma Ineson and Cara Lovell for their invitation and for the soon-to-be priests for their generous engagement with a prayer which was unfamiliar to most of them. They encouraged me that this was a prayer which could speak to a new generation of Christians just as powerfully as it has done in the past.

I am grateful to my alma mater, St John's College, Durham, for allowing me to use their wonderful library to research and to write and to Rachel and Duncan Ross-Russell for letting me use their flat in North Yorkshire as a place to hide away and type.

My parents, Ann and Lionel Plyming, continue to be for me a model of thankful living. They are attentive to God's daily mercies and write the most wonderful thank you letters. If I have picked up any good habits of giving thanks over the years, it is from them.

Annabelle, my wife, shows me how gratitude is at the heart of a loving relationship. I am so grateful for her support of me in the transition to ministry at the Cathedral, and I also give thanks for her own precious ministry working in palliative medicine. How she found time to check a final copy of this manuscript is beyond me.

I also want to thank my two sons, Sam and James. Despite what I say in the Introduction, they are actually very good at expressing appreciation, and I in turn want to thank them for their support, kindness and willingness to watch sports fixtures with me. They have made the responsibility of parenting something for which I am very thankful.

The staff at Canterbury Press have once again been a model of encouragement and efficiency. I am grateful to David Sherving-

ACKNOWLEDGEMENTS

ton, Natalie Quinn and Kate Hughes for all their support and wisdom in bringing this book to publication.

I dedicate this book to the community at Durham Cathedral, staff, volunteers and members of the worshipping community. It is offered in thanksgiving for the privilege of leading the life and mission of Durham Cathedral, and with the prayer that we will all be drawn deeper into the inestimable love of God and show forth God's praise not only with our lips but in our lives.

Philip Plyming
Durham Cathedral
Petertide, June 2025

Introduction – Let's Give Thanks

No one told me that thank you letters would be the toughest test of my parenting skills.

Not the sleepless nights or the toddler tantrums. Not the early morning music practice or supervising homework. No, what took me to breaking point (and beyond, if you ask my children) was the exercise after Christmas each year of getting my two sons to write thank you letters to all the people who had given them presents. I held off until the day after Boxing Day but then I reminded them (gently at first) that the letters needed to be written, and that, yes, they did need to be handwritten, and yes, they did need to be personal and no, I wasn't going to write the envelopes. There were usually tears before the whole exercise was finished just in time for Lent.

It was some small comfort that other parents told me of similar experiences. We shared both a strong sense that our children needed to learn to express thanks for the many presents they had received and also what felt like a mountain to climb in terms of getting our children to see the point of it all.

I continue to write thank you letters – after invitations to dinner, after staying with friends, after outstanding work from colleagues – but from looking at the generation below me I sometimes fear that saying thank you is on the way out.

The rise of thankfulness

Only it isn't. Because, within the worlds of both popular psychology and academic study, thankfulness is on the march. Brother David Steindl-Rast, a Benedictine monk and creator of the worldwide movement 'A Network for Grateful Living', talks about a 'gratitude boom' in which scientific research is creating a feedback loop that strengthens popular interest in the practice of thankfulness.[1]

Robert Emmons, a key scholar in this area, has defined gratitude as having two components: first, 'an affirmation that there are good things in the world, things from which we have benefited', and second, 'a recognition of where that goodness comes from – the people and things in our life that have conspired to give it to us'.[2]

Both these components are seen in the popular interest in thankfulness, which has grown out of and alongside mindfulness in contemporary self-help culture. This growth is evidenced in the plethora of materials for those who want to practise gratitude: there are gratitude journals to buy, gratitude cards to write, ten tips to practise daily gratitude and advice on practising a five-minute gratitude meditation, using all your senses to help you give thanks.[3]

However, as Steindl-Rast notes, it is the growth in scientific studies that has really fuelled the rediscovery of what Cicero 2,000 years ago described as 'not only the greatest one but also the mother of all the other remaining virtues'. In 2001 Robert Emmons set up the Greater Good Science Center at the University of California, Berkeley, to explore 'the science of a meaningful life', and since 2014 this centre has distributed $4 million to researchers looking at the science and practice of gratitude. Their studies have explored how thankfulness is impacted by our genes, our brains, our gender and our cultural background, and they have also sought to assess the benefits of gratitude for individuals and wider society.

---

1 Jill Suttie, 2020, 'Is gratitude the path to a better world?' in Jeremy Adam Smith, Kira M. Newman, Jason Marsh and Dacher Keltner (eds), *The Gratitude Project: How the Science of Thankfulness Can Rewire Our Brains for Resilience, Optimism and the Greater Good*, Oakland, CA: New Harbinger Publications, p. 197.

2 Robert Emmons and Jeremy Adam Smith, 2020, 'What gratitude is and why it matters' in Smith et al. (eds), *The Gratitude Project*, pp. 5–6.

3 Mindful, n.d., 'How to Practice Gratitude', www.mindful.org/an-introduction-to-mindful-gratitude, accessed 25.04.2025.

INTRODUCTION – LET'S GIVE THANKS

In terms of individuals, it has been argued that there is now scientific evidence to support the claim that the practice of gratitude helps us get more out of life. This is the bold claim: 'Practicing gratitude has proven to be one of the most reliable methods for increasing happiness and life satisfaction; it also boosts feelings of optimism, joy, pleasure, enthusiasm and other positive emotions.'[4] Crucially, it is also said to help deliver positive outcomes for those struggling with their mental health, with evidence suggesting that 'practicing gratitude on top of receiving psychological counselling carries greater benefits than having counselling alone'.[5]

Practising gratitude is also good for society. It has been found to increase levels of generosity, nurture prosocial behaviour such as helpfulness and humility, strengthen relationships and reinforce cultural bonds that remind us we need one another.[6]

During the early stages of the Covid-19 pandemic I stood on our doorstep most Thursday evenings at 8pm and banged a saucepan with a wooden spoon. It was my contribution to 'Clap for Carers', an initiative to express the nation's thanks to those who were looking after us during the dark days of the pandemic. We could hear and see people doing likewise in our Durham street, and as we practised gratitude in that way we expressed that we belonged together and shared a dependence on others.

Thankfulness is good for us as individuals and for our society.

Is thankfulness that good?

But that last example opens up a tougher question about thankfulness. Because if you ask many NHS staff how they look back on 'Clap for Carers' now, their views are mixed. They appreciated it at the time, but are disappointed that it was not followed up

---

4 Joel Wong, Joshua Brown, Christina Armenta, Sonja Lyubomirsky, Summer Allen, Amie Gordon and Kira Newman, 'Why gratitude is good for us' in Smith et al. (eds), *The Gratitude Project*, p. 39.

5 Wong et al., 'Why gratitude is good for us', p. 40.

6 Emmons and Smith, 'What gratitude is and why it matters', p. 4.

with action to support the NHS as it tried to get on its feet after the lockdowns finished.

Thankfulness has its critics as well. Some think that it reinforces inequality by making people give thanks for the little they have rather than challenging the systems which keep them in poverty.[7] Others argue that practising gratitude requires a level of denial of reality, because it filters out the really tough bits of life. A mother who practised gratitude while caring for a son with life-threatening health needs was asked on BBC Radio 4's *Moral Maze* if she wasn't simply pretending that life was great when it patently wasn't. And few who saw it will forget the scene in the Oval Office when Ukrainian President Volodymyr Zelensky was berated by Vice-President J. D. Vance for not being grateful enough to the USA for the military and financial support they had been given. Here thankfulness was being weaponized to reinforce a feeling of subservience. It made for very uncomfortable viewing.

Indeed, we have to ask whether it is really appropriate to focus on giving thanks as the world enters the second quarter of the twenty-first century. The California of the early 2000s might have been fertile ground for considering the benefits of gratitude, but with the world order facing unprecedented changes and challenges, with social and economic pressures in the UK greater than for decades, let alone the personal trials many of us may be living through, including with our own mental health, we have to ask whether giving thanks is not best kept for another day. Perhaps when things are looking up again, then we can put gratitude back on the agenda.

Giving thanks in all circumstances

So far, I have kept faith on the back burner of this discussion, but it can't stay there. Because for all of us who are seeking in any way to follow Jesus Christ and walk the way of faith, not giving thanks isn't really an option. When the Apostle Paul writes to

---

7 Emmons and Smith, 'What gratitude is and why it matters', p. 3.

INTRODUCTION – LET'S GIVE THANKS

the young church in Thessaloniki, in what is possibly the earliest piece of extant Christian communication, 'Rejoice always, pray without ceasing, give thanks in all circumstances; for this is the will of God in Christ Jesus for you' (1 Thess. 5.16–18), this does not seem specific advice for that Christian community alone. Rather, the call to 'give thanks in all circumstances' is one that would seem to press on every follower of Jesus seeking to be faithful in their walk with the Lord.

It can be easily noted, of course, that Paul does not command us to give thanks *for* all circumstances; we are not required to thank God when horrible things happen to us and to others. But that doesn't take away from the challenge, because we are still left with the demanding question of what giving thanks *in all circumstances* actually looks like. Does it mean seeing the silver lining to every cloud? Does it mean screwing up our eyes and believing that, in the words of Captain Sir Tom Moore, 'Tomorrow will be a better day'? Is giving thanks in all circumstances another of those biblical principles which just reinforce a sense that we are not very good Christians?

We may welcome the evidence that suggests that giving thanks is good for us and for society, but we need to ensure that this practice is firmly rooted not simply in contemporary psychology but also in a deep understanding of Christian faith. Indeed, we will want to ask some important questions about what giving thanks really involves.

- How does a distinctively Christian way of seeing both God and ourselves give us the resources to give thanks every day?
- How is giving thanks not simply a duty but rather something that can overflow from an appreciation of the good news of God in Jesus Christ?
- How do we give thanks when the world around us appears to be falling apart?
- How does giving thanks involve not just a prayer journal but our whole lives?
- How is giving thanks good for us and our walk with the Lord?

These questions are what this book is about.

The General Thanksgiving

Now it would be possible to explore these questions by going back to the Apostle Paul's letters to the Thessalonians and elsewhere and seeing what he really meant. But I am going to suggest we look somewhere else, albeit somewhere inspired by another verse from Paul. Because when Paul writes to the Colossians, 'Devote yourselves to prayer, keeping alert in it with thanksgiving' (Col. 4.2) he invites us to see giving thanks as something primarily rooted in prayer, something that is done not as a one-off but as a regular discipline of gratitude.

There is one prayer that fits the bill perfectly. Written over 350 years ago, it is still in print today because it forms part of the Book of Common Prayer (commonly known as the BCP), part of the official set of worship services of the Church of England. It is known as the General Thanksgiving.

Now you may or may not know the General Thanksgiving already (and if you don't, this book is particularly aimed at you). But I can tell you from my ministry over the last 25 years that this prayer has been known and prayed by generations of followers of Jesus Christ. In the parish where I was vicar many of the older people had learned the General Thanksgiving off by heart as part of their confirmation preparation (together with the Lord's Prayer and the Apostles' Creed). These were people who had lived through and said the prayer during tough times such as the trials of World War Two. Now many years later they would join in with me if I ended a prayer time with it during a home visit. Amid health challenges and family concerns, it was a prayer that helped them to give thanks.

It is a prayer I have come to know and love over the years. I use it when I lead prayers in services at Durham Cathedral and I use it in my own personal prayer times, particularly when things are tough and I am finding it hard to pray. It is quite simply one of my very favourite prayers and as I have prayed it regularly over the years I have found that, like all good prayers, it has changed me and moulded me to be someone who is more attentive and thankful for God's mercies great and small.

This book is an invitation for us to explore this wonderful

INTRODUCTION – LET'S GIVE THANKS

prayer together. Because my belief is that, though some of the language in this prayer is a little old-fashioned, its shape and message are exactly what we need to hear today. Indeed, I think that as we look at this prayer carefully together we will get to the heart of what giving thanks is all about.

If you are someone who is new to faith or still exploring what faith is all about, I hope this book will help you see the wonderful news of God's love in Jesus Christ and invite you to see the Christian life not as a set of duties but instead a wholehearted response of giving thanks to the God who made us and loves us.

If you find giving thanks hard or frankly beyond you at the moment, I hope this book will give you words to both inhabit and pray which help us look beyond ourselves to the God who is faithful and merciful. You don't have to feel guilty that you can't find the words to pray; here are words for you that you can whisper with the saints of every age.

If you pick up this book to read during Lent, I hope it helps you to explore new ways of praying and going deeper with the Lord, and to prepare to celebrate Easter with lasting thanks in your heart. I am going to suggest at the end that you can learn the prayer off by heart – now there's a good Lenten discipline!

And if you are already a superfan of the General Thanksgiving and the Book of Common Prayer, I hope this book highlights some aspects of the prayer that you haven't seen before and enables you to pray it with even greater faith. You won't need convincing that the General Thanksgiving and the Book of Common Prayer are a wonderful resource for faith today – but enjoy the ride anyway!

You will notice that Durham Cathedral crops up quite a few times in the book. This is probably inevitable because I find as Dean that worshipping and praying daily in the cathedral informs and enriches my experience of God. If you know the cathedral well, you will be able to imagine where I am referring to. If you haven't been, I hope one of the by-products of reading this book is that you will want to come!

A final word of prior warning: a couple of times in the book I refer to the impact of the sexual abuse I suffered as a child, something which I wrote a little about in my book *Being Real*.[8] I don't go into any details in this book, but if you are someone who would value knowing in advance that this topic is going to come up, I hope this is helpful.

A thankful journey

So let's prepare to go on this journey of giving thanks together. The General Thanksgiving provides the overall shape of this book, which is in three parts.

Part One is all about getting started, with the prayer itself, with God, with ourselves and with some initial reasons for giving thanks.

First (in Chapter 1), we will introduce the General Thanksgiving and tell the fascinating story of Edward Reynolds, the man who wrote it, and how it came to be included in the Book of Common Prayer right at the last moment. We will see that the prayer was written at a time of great turmoil in people's lives, when giving thanks would have been a demanding calling indeed. If we are going through tough times today, we need to know that the General Thanksgiving was not written just for the good times.

Second (in Chapter 2), we will start looking at the prayer and in particular the God to whom it is addressed. Modern studies on gratitude leave the identity of any divine being who is being thanked largely unexplored, but the General Thanksgiving names who God is and helps us come to a God who is both mighty and merciful. In the light of who we are – both beautiful and broken – that is good news indeed and means we can pray without shame.

Third (in Chapter 3), we will then look at some everyday reasons to give thanks. We will see how simply being made is a reason to thank God, as is being sustained in daily life. Indeed, recognizing all that we have as blessings can go a long way to moving our hearts to thanksgiving.

---

8 Philip Plyming, 2023, *Being Real: The Apostle Paul's Hardship Narratives and The Stories We Tell Today*, London: SCM Press.

INTRODUCTION – LET'S GIVE THANKS

Part Two takes us to the heart of the prayer and indeed our own thanksgiving – namely, the wonderful, described as 'inestimable', love of God.

First (in Chapter 4), we will look at this love poured out in the past as we consider what it means to thank God for the 'redemption of the world in our Lord Jesus Christ'. We will see how the death of Jesus on the cross is God's great act of freedom for the world, and also an assurance that as well as being 'beautiful and broken' we are also loved. Whatever else we give thanks for, we can give thanks for God's love poured out on the cross.

Second (in Chapter 5), we will look at God's love in the present as we explore the phrase 'the means of grace'. We will see how God has given us ways to experience his love and presence every day; as we enjoy the Bible, prayer and Holy Communion as ways to meet with God in our daily lives, we find in them not reasons to be guilty but sources of heartfelt thanks.

Third (in Chapter 6), we will look at God's love in the future as we consider the phrase 'the hope of glory'. We will look together at what this glory is and how it helps us both to know Christ with us in the present and to look death in the face without fear. In the light of this, as we will see with the story of St Cuthbert, we will be able to give thanks in the most unpromising of circumstances.

Part Three is about the 'so what' of giving thanks. The General Thanksgiving invites us to see giving thanks as a much more wholehearted endeavour than simply filling in a gratitude journal. It involves everything we are, say and do.

First (in Chapter 7), we will look at what it means to nurture a thankful heart. We will explore how the human heart is actually the locus for all our decision-making and see that hearts that are proud and stubborn will struggle to respond in thanks to God, whereas hearts that are humble and open can see reasons to give thanks in unlikely places.

Second (in Chapter 8), we will consider what it looks like to live a thankful life. We will see how it is less what we say and more what we do that marks a truly thankful life, and how giving up ourselves and serving God and others is not the path to less joy but actually to the real reason we were made. And we will see how the call to holiness is not about cold duty but heartfelt love.

Third (in Chapter 9), we will consider what it means to give thanks to God not for our benefit, but for God's lasting glory. We will see how giving thanks to God helps us see ourselves in the right light as well as those who dominate the world stage today. And giving thanks to God reminds us that God's story stretches to the end of the age. Our giving thanks is part of a much bigger story.

At the heart of the prayer and this book is this simple message: giving thanks to God is good for us.

Come with me and see how.

PART I

Getting Started: Foundations for a Thankful Life

I

A Pioneering Prayer: Introducing the General Thanksgiving

Perhaps like me you have popped into an old church while on holiday – perhaps to see inside, or perhaps to dodge a shower. If you have done this, you know that when you go into an old church, there are certain things you usually find. A guide to the building showing which bits were constructed when. A visitor's book with some appreciative comments in it. A box (or now often a machine) to leave a donation. And then at the back, by the hymn books, there are a shelf or two of dark small books arranged neatly in a row. If you go closer you can see they have the words 'Book of Common Prayer' on the spine. And if you pick them up, they often have dust on them and an unmistakable old book smell about them.

Because this is the first experience of, or introduction to, the Book of Common Prayer that many people have, it is easy to come to the view that this is, and always has been, an old-fashioned book whose day has long passed. But this is to misunderstand how innovative and controversial the Book of Common Prayer was when it was first introduced, and how it was, for quite some time, a book that was challenged and questioned more than any other book in these lands.

If we are going to understand and appreciate (and use) the prayer we know as the General Thanksgiving, we need to understand how the Book of Common Prayer came to be written and the extraordinary story of how this particular prayer only narrowly made it in.

A controversial book

We may be aware that the Church of England was established in the reign of Henry VIII, who for personal reasons wanted to break away from the control of the Pope in Rome. What is less well known is that right up to the end of Henry's reign in 1547 the worship in churches throughout England stayed largely the same. Yes, there was now a Bible in each church (the Great Bible had been authorized in 1539 and copies were to be placed in every church), but the services were as they had always been.

The real changes in how people worshipped came after Henry died and his son Edward VI came to the throne. Although he was only nine when he became king, his advisers were all thoroughly Protestant in nature. Thomas Cranmer, whom Henry had appointed as Archbishop of Canterbury but who had always felt constrained in what he could alter, now felt that he had the support to make some really radical changes.

The Book of Common Prayer was that radical change. Largely written by Cranmer himself, the first edition came out in 1549 and was the first book of services which was a) for all churches to use and b) entirely in English as opposed to Latin. Cranmer also took some decisive steps away from a Catholic understanding of worship to a more Protestant one. From 9 June 1549 all churches had to use the Book of Common Prayer for their public worship.

It may be difficult to believe now, but the publication and enforcement of the new Prayer Book resulted in riots and open rebellion. This was especially the case in Devon and Cornwall, where Catholic sentiment was strong and people resented having to worship in English (when Cornish was often the mother tongue). Battles were fought, the city of Exeter was besieged for five weeks and over 5,500 people died. And all over a book we now see as rather dusty and old-fashioned.

The controversy continued. Thomas Cranmer issued a revised version of the Book of Common Prayer in 1552 which was more Protestant in nature, but within a year Edward VI died and Catholic Queen Mary came to the throne, banning the new Prayer Book from churches, reinstating the Latin Mass and eventually having Archbishop Cranmer burned at the stake.

A PIONEERING PRAYER

Elizabeth I reissued the Prayer Book in 1559, although even this was accompanied by lots of arguments about specific words and phrases, controversies which were re-run when a further edition was made in 1604.

And the Book of Common Prayer was to be banned one more time. With the Civil War in the 1640s came the victory of the Parliamentarians, many of whom were Puritan in conviction and who regarded the Book of Common Prayer with distrust. And so in 1645 the Book of Common Prayer was outlawed by Parliament and replaced by another book, more informal in nature, called the Directory of Public Worship. The Book of Common Prayer wasn't made legal again until 1660 and the restoration of the monarchy under Charles II.

So in just over 100 years the Book of Common Prayer had gone through four editions and been banned twice. This was a book that divided opinion.

The man behind the prayer

There was a further decisive chapter of the Book of Common Prayer to be written, and here we meet the man behind the Prayer of General Thanksgiving, Edward Reynolds himself. His story is both remarkable and points to the fraught and painful times in which he lived.

Reynolds was born in Southampton in 1599 and showed himself at an early age to be a fine scholar, taking his degree at Oxford. His first job after ordination at the age of 23 was as preacher at Lincoln's Inn in London, where he took over from the renowned John Donne. After nine years he moved to Braunston in Northamptonshire where he was vicar when the Civil War broke out.

Like a number of clergy, Edward Reynolds was happy to side with the Parliamentarian forces and continued his pastoral ministry without the oversight of a bishop. For a while he became a leading light in the Presbyterian Church, attending the Westminster Assembly in 1643; he was made Dean of Christ Church Oxford and Vice-Chancellor of the University in 1648. Yet he was no hardline radical and refused to take part in some of the more extreme steps of the Presbyterian Church, such as making use of the Book of Common Prayer illegal. He lost his jobs in Oxford and returned to Northamptonshire before securing a post in a parish in London, where over time he increasingly spoke out in favour of moderation and tolerance in religious matters.

Given what the country had been through over the previous 20 years, such calls were entirely understandable. For while Reynolds had simply lost his jobs amid all the political turmoil, others had fared much worse. In a brilliant study of the 11 years when England was without a king, historian Anna Keay depicts stories from a 'post-war land scarred by conflict and its monumental cost – human, material and financial'.[1] Up to 5% of the population had died in the Civil War, the same proportion as in World War One. Families had been torn apart and communities ruined. And this was on top of the fragility of human life, with one-fifth of all children dying before their first birthday. For those who survived, life expectancy was significantly lower than it is today.

It is worth noting at this stage that these were not auspicious times to be writing a prayer of thanksgiving. Life for many people was both hard and uncertain.

A restoration conference

Edward Reynolds was ministering in London when Charles II returned to England in 1660 and took the crown. King Charles clearly thought highly of him and made him Bishop of Norwich before the year was out. The stage was set for Reynolds's finest hour.

Soon after his restoration Charles II had sought to tackle one of the tasks at the top of his to-do list, which was to bring unity to what was a divided Church. In particular, he wanted to see if some reconciliation could be achieved between the bishops of the Church of England (who had been recently restored to their posts) and those representing the Puritan and Presbyterian traditions which had until recently held sway under the Commonwealth.

---

1 Anna Keay, 2023, *The Restless Republic: Britain without a Crown*, London: HarperCollins, p. xiv.

The focus of discussion was the Book of Common Prayer itself, which the bishops wanted reinstated in full and which the Presbyterians thought deficient in a number of places.

Charles's solution was to call a conference to bring the differing parties together. Called the Savoy Conference (because it took place at a grand house in London called the Savoy Hospital), it brought together in the same room 12 bishops and 12 leaders of the Presbyterian Church, one of whom was a bishop. You've guessed it: it was Edward Reynolds.

Just imagine the scene: here was a bishop lining up against 12 of his colleagues. He was trying to get them to take seriously the complaints (called Great Exceptions) that the Presbyterians had about the Book of Common Prayer. One of their complaints was that the prayers in the Book of Common Prayer were too short and rigid. They wanted prayers that were longer and more clearly from the heart.

The Savoy Conference lasted for four months but it was clear long before it ended that it was going to be a complete failure. The bishops were in no mood to compromise. With Charles II behind them they held all the power and any concessions they made were token in nature. The Presbyterians got virtually nothing of what they wanted. It was clear that there was to be no accommodation of them in the national Church.

The eleventh hour

And yet Reynolds did not give up. Despite his undoubted distress at the failure of the Savoy Conference and the threat that many of his Presbyterian colleagues would have to leave the Church of England, he still had one card left to play. Unlike his Presbyterian colleagues at the Savoy Conference, he was a serving bishop and so still had a role in agreeing the new Book of Common Prayer that Charles wanted to issue in 1662. The revised Book of Common Prayer would need to be agreed by the House of Bishops – that is, bishops including Reynolds. And so, as 1661 drew to a close, Reynolds had a plan. He was going to get a new prayer accepted and inserted at the very last minute.

How long the plan had been in the making we don't really know. Like many set prayers it uses phrases that have been used elsewhere, and other people were invited to comment on it and make their own suggestions. Scholars have found phrases from the General Thanksgiving in all sorts of places, including in a personal prayer of Queen Elizabeth I from 1574.[2] It seems likely that Robert Sanderson, Bishop of Lincoln, made some comments as well.[3] But certainly Edward Reynolds was the one who pulled it all together. Perhaps after the disappointment of the Savoy Conference he tidied up the prayer he had been working on for a while and got ready to submit it.

And here, it would seem, he broke the rules. New prayers were not simply meant to be offered up for inclusion in the revised Book of Common Prayer. They were properly to be requested by the House of Bishops, but it seems that they had not asked for a new prayer of thanksgiving, general or otherwise. There were already brief prayers of thanksgiving for specific situations (rain, fair weather and deliverance from enemies to name just three) and it would seem that the bishops thought that was enough.

Also, new prayers were meant to be discussed and revised in committee before they were introduced to all the bishops. This would enable detailed textual work to be done so that plenary time was not wasted. Again, it seems that Reynolds did not go down this route. He was playing a high stakes game. He realized that he couldn't get all the changes that his Presbyterian colleagues wanted. But if he could get one change through, that might win over some of his moderate clergy friends and make the split in the Church slightly less drastic. It was perhaps a token effort, but it was worth a try.

So, it was at eight o'clock on the morning of Saturday 14 December 1661 that Edward Reynolds, the Presbyterian bishop, introduced the General Thanksgiving to a meeting of the House of Bishops – that is, all his senior colleagues. First, he read the

---

2 Marion J. Hatchett, 1995, *Commentary on the American Prayer Book*, San Francisco, CA: HarperCollins, p. 130.

3 For a detailed account of the creation of the General Thanksgiving, see G. J. Cuming, 1983, *The Godly Order: Texts and Studies Relating to the Book of Common Prayer*, London: Alcuin Club, pp. 152–62.

prayer out, no doubt quite carefully so that the rhythm and scan of the prayer could be well appreciated. And then he sat back for comment. For two hours the bishops discussed the prayer, a sign that they were not prepared for it to go through on the nod. And then at ten o'clock they approved it.

Just six days later, on 20 December 1661, the final version of the Prayer Book was signed on behalf of the House of Bishops, ready for printing early in the New Year and its formal adoption on 14 August 1662. The Prayer of General Thanksgiving – now one of the most loved and popular of all the prayers in the Book of Common Prayer – had made it in by the skin of its teeth.

The shape of the General Thanksgiving

None of this, of course, is clear when you read the General Thanksgiving in any edition produced in 1662 or since (and it is still very much in print today). In the wonderful library at Durham Cathedral we have a first edition of the 1662 Book of Common Prayer, and I was able to handle it and read the General Thanksgiving as it appeared when it was first published. The prayer is slightly tucked away at the bottom of a page in a section called Prayers and Thanksgivings, which is squeezed in between Morning and Evening Prayer and then the Collects and Bible readings for each Sunday of the Church's year. It is more than a little tricky to find.

What is also hard to discern is the overall shape of the prayer, not least because it is printed as continuous text over two columns of a book the size of a modern paperback. This is a shame because, as you might imagine, the prayer is very carefully constructed and serves not only as a beautiful prayer in itself but also as a model for the journey of thanksgiving that this book is all about. Here the Presbyterian in Edward Reynolds might be coming out, writing a prayer that was not simply to be said by rote but could also be improvised on, with people using the basic structure as a framework.

Therefore, before we look at the prayer in detail and think about how it can assist us to grow in gratitude, I want to help us get a feel for the prayer as a whole. If we break it down into sections, it could look like this:

ALMIGHTY God, Father of all mercies,
We thine unworthy servants
do give thee most humble and hearty thanks
for all thy goodness and loving-kindness to us and to all men;
(particularly to those who desire now to offer up their praises and thanksgivings for thy late mercies vouchsafed unto them)

We bless thee for our
creation,
preservation,
and all the blessings of this life;
but above all
for thine inestimable love in the redemption of the world
  by our Lord Jesus Christ,
for the means of grace,
and for the hope of glory.

And we beseech thee,
give us that due sense of all thy mercies,
that our hearts may be unfeignedly thankful,
and that we shew forth thy praise,
not only with our lips, but in our lives;
by giving up ourselves to thy service,
and by walking before thee
in holiness and righteousness all our days;

through Jesus Christ our Lord,
to whom with thee and the Holy Ghost be all honour
  and glory,
world without end. **Amen.**

In setting out the prayer in this way, we can note a couple of things.

First, there is an introductory sentence which names who is involved in the prayer (God and us) and says something about the relationship between the two. The phrase in brackets and italics is printed like this in the original, and we will come back to this later.

There is then a sentence that focuses on reasons for thanksgiving, both general (creation, preservation and all the blessings of this life) and specifically Christian (inestimable love in redemption, means of grace and hope of glory). All of these important words will be explored in future chapters.

The final sentence of the prayer focuses on the worshipper's response. It is still a prayer ('we beseech thee') but it hones in on what it is to give thanks not simply with our lips but also in our lives. In other words, it is about the 'so what' of giving thanks. What difference does giving thanks make to what we do each day?

It is thus a beautifully balanced prayer. It concerns both God and us. It explores both reasons to give thanks, and also the practical outworking of those thanks. It is both general and specific. It is both formal, and open to personal expansion.

A word here about language. It is quite possible that as you read the prayer a couple of things were a little off-putting. First, the use of 'thee', 'thy' and 'thine' which, while quite normal in the seventeenth century, are not words we use today. People make different calls on this today: some prefer to convert such terms into 'you' and 'your' (and in the Appendix to this book there is a version of this prayer which does just that), while others, including myself, quite like these words as an intimate way of speaking with God. A prayer language, if you like. You choose whatever works for you, but as a rule this book will deal with Edwards Reynolds's original version.

The second concern is over certain words whose meaning is perhaps not clear. 'Inestimable' and 'unfeignedly' are the two obvious ones, but we also might not be sure what preservation is all about and what righteousness really involves. Don't worry, you are not alone, and I will explain each of these terms when we come across them.

A hearty prayer

The poet Malcolm Guite, writing on the General Thanksgiving, takes as his inspiration the word 'hearty' and imagines the prayer as a culinary event. He writes:

> If thanksgivings were breakfasts, then the General Thanksgiving would not be some slender option with a little muesli and a couple of grapes; no, it would be 'The Full English'! It manages to get generous helpings of almost everything on to the plate; for it is the least stingy, the most inclusive of prayers. I love all its *alls*: '*all* mercies', '*all* thy goodness and loving-kindness to us and to *all* men', '*all* the blessings of this life', '*all* honour and glory'.[4]

And he concludes:

> When it comes to breakfast you can, I regret to say, have too much of a good thing, but you can never have too much thanksgiving. A hearty breakfast might leave you a little weighted and ponderous, but a hearty thanksgiving tends to lighten your step, and give you edge and appetite for all that the day might bring.[5]

So, let's begin our meal, and see who is sitting at the table with us.

---

4 Malcolm Guite, 2018, 'Malcolm Guite relishes the General Thanksgiving, the "Full English" of prayers', *Church Times*, https://www.churchtimes.co.uk/articles/2018/2-march/comment/columnists/malcolm-guite-poet-s-corner, accessed 24.04.2025.

5 Guite, 'Malcolm Guite relishes the General Thanksgiving, the "Full English" of prayers'.

2

Who's on the Call?
Seeing God and Ourselves Clearly

*'Almighty God, Father of all mercies,
we thine unworthy servants'*

At work now I very rarely make phone calls. If I need to have a conversation with someone who is not in the Cathedral precinct, I don't contact them via my landline or mobile. I set up a Teams call or invite them to my Zoom room. And we chat face to face, with or without blurred background.

I think this is one of the ways the pandemic lockdowns changed things on what feels like a permanent basis. Before Covid-19 I was used to setting up phone meetings, but once I learned how to use Teams and Zoom (by one of my colleagues very patiently teaching me) I realized it was so much better to see the person I was talking to.

Recently I was doing a mentoring session for a colleague elsewhere in the country. Her wi-fi went down and we had to speak for an hour on the phone. I was reminded how hard it was to speak to someone if you can't see their face. It feels much harder to know how they are feeling, and therefore how you should speak in response.

We want to know who we are speaking to. And a picture makes that so much easier.

I think there is a similar dynamic at work in prayer. It is important for prayer in the Christian tradition that we know who we are speaking to. Our words are not offered up into an empty space nor to a God who is hidden behind a cloud of unknowing. Neither are we praying to a God who is made in our image, as if we can make God into whoever we want God to be.

The truth is that, while we can't see God on a Teams call, in Scripture we are given a picture of who God is and therefore who we are praying to. At Durham Cathedral we continue Cranmer's tradition of reading or singing through all the Psalms on a regular cycle. And one of the things that strikes me again and again is the way that these great songs and prayers take time to describe who God is, as if getting our picture of God right is crucial to setting our praise and prayer on a secure footing. That picture is then enhanced in our New Testament readings, which reflect God supremely revealed in the face of Jesus Christ.

When he wrote the General Thanksgiving, Edward Reynolds took this pattern to heart. His prayer starts with a twofold description of who God is (the first description quite expected, the second much less so) and also a narration of who we are (and that is really quite unusual). As we look at what it means for us to pray prayers and live lives of giving thanks, we need to be very clear about the God who is being thanked, and who is doing the thanking.

Almighty God

The prayer starts by addressing God as 'Almighty God'. This was not unusual. The Book of Common Prayer, for which Reynolds was writing, includes a number of set prayers called Collects for each Sunday of the year. Many of them were written by Thomas Cranmer, albeit often drawing on previous versions, and each of them starts with addressing God in a particular way. By far the most common way to address God is 'Almighty God'. But what does it mean for us to address God in this way?

It is a phrase that speaks primarily of God's power. It recognizes that God has unlimited agency over all creation and that nothing comes close to God's strength.

There are references to 'the Almighty' or 'God Almighty' throughout Scripture, but probably the best place to go for a description of God as Almighty is in a passage that doesn't actually use the word but expounds it with an intensity that is deeply moving. It comes from the moment when King David has gathered together offerings and donations for the building of the new Temple in Jerusalem and is preparing to dedicate them to the Lord. The beginning of his prayer includes these words:

> Blessed are you, O LORD, the God of our ancestor Israel, for ever and ever. Yours, O LORD, are the greatness, the power, the glory, the victory, and the majesty; for all that is in the heavens and on the earth is yours; yours is the kingdom, O LORD, and you are exalted as head above all. Riches and honour come from you, and you rule over all. In your hand are power and might; and it is in your hand to make great and to give strength to all. (1 Chron. 29.10–12)

As well as drinking in the poetry of David's prayer, there are several things to spot here that are evidence of God's power.

First, there is power seen in creation. Believing that all of creation is the work of God's hand can but lead us to see God as Almighty. I love walking in Scotland, and one of the things I do when I reach the top of a peak is look out over the hills and think to myself, 'God made this.'

Second, there is power seen over rulers. King David recognizes that there is someone who holds authority over him. He is not in complete charge. However permanent rulers and dynasties may feel (and some feel pretty permanent at the moment), history teaches us that they do not have ultimate control over their own destiny. Only God's kingdom lasts.

Third, there is power that lasts over time. David praises God who is blessed for ever and ever. One of the toughest things to get our heads around is that God has power over time itself, because God is outside time. It is striking that one of the books of the Bible that uses the word 'Almighty' most is the final book, Revelation, which was written at a time when it seemed as if the secular powers were in absolute charge. But John's vision includes a description of the Almighty who is the beginning and end of all things: '"I am the Alpha and Omega", says the Lord God, who is and who was and who is to come, the Almighty' (Rev. 1.8). God's power is over time itself. This is God Almighty.

One of the things people always notice about Durham Cathedral when they visit is the stone pillars. They are massive – 6.6 metres round and 6.6 metres high. Once you have seen them you never forget them. They present a picture of durability and strength which understandably evokes a sense of awe. However, when I look at them and appreciate them, I am reminded that they are nothing put alongside the Almighty God, the God who shaped the Milky Way, defeated Pharaoh and was there before the Big Bang. If I am awed by the size of the pillars, how much more can I be awed by the living and reigning God Almighty.

Father of all mercies

So far, so standard. Addressing God as 'Almighty God' was normal for both the biblical writers and the writers of Reynolds's time. But Reynolds does not leave it there. He follows up with another form of address to God – Father of all mercies – and here we are on some really interesting ground.

'Father', of course, should come as no surprise to any of us who pray the Lord's Prayer on a regular basis. 'Our Father', Jesus taught his disciples to pray, and the Apostle Paul rejoices that being able to call God 'Abba, Father' is one of the great blessings of the Spirit-filled life (Rom. 8.15–16). It denotes both intimacy and respect, rather as my sons when they were little would start a sentence with 'Daddy' before continuing with an unanswerable question or an argument about why they shouldn't go to bed. Being able to call God 'Father' is a privilege we should never take for granted.

But 'Father of all mercies' is something else. It is a phrase which is not there in that exact form in the Bible, but the passage which is closest to it gets us to the heart of what it is all about, 'Blessed be the God and Father of our Lord Jesus Christ, the Father of mercies and God of all consolation' (2 Cor. 1.3).

Writing what we call his second letter to the church in Corinth, the Apostle Paul begins with a profound reflection on what he has experienced of God through his recent time of suffering and trial (he doesn't go into the details, other than that it happened in Asia). And the overall message is this: God has come alongside him in tenderness and care. He writes what is essentially an extended riff on the word *parakaleo*, which can be translated 'console' or 'comfort', and his point is this: he prays that the consolation he has received from God in Christ will be true for the Corinthian believers as well.

This is the 'Father of mercies' that Paul addresses in his opening benediction. It is a God who has not remained distant and aloof but a God whom Paul has known as close and caring. We don't know exactly how this was manifested but we can trust that bit was real. Paul was in a hole, but he found he wasn't alone.

When I think of the phrase 'Father of all mercies' (Reynolds adds an 'all' into the middle of Paul's phrase to make it yet more powerful), I am reminded of the famous Rembrandt picture of the Parable of the Prodigal Son, and the father tenderly embracing the younger son and placing his hands on his back. When I went to see the picture in the Hermitage in St Petersburg I looked at the hands close up, because I had read that one was modelled on a male hand and the other on a female hand. And that may well be true but what struck me was just the tenderness with which both hands were touching the son. Compared to so many expressions of power in the political sphere today, this was a father expressing his power with gentleness and warmth. This was a father of all mercies.

Such mercies will be the very stuff of the prayer that follows. We will be invited to thank God for all God's mercies to us, the nature of which we shall look at in the coming chapters. And we will ask God to make those mercies thoroughly vivid and present to us. But for now we can just note and let it sink in that the God we are giving thanks to is a giver of compassionate gifts, a Father of all mercies.

A 'both/and' God

This is the God to whom we are going to be invited to give thanks, a God who is both almighty and also the Father of all mercies. A God who is powerful but also tender, a God who has unlimited agency but expresses it in works of comfort and care.

And as we go through the journey of praying this prayer

together, we will need to keep both these views of God in mind. It may be that we find one more naturally attractive than the other. Perhaps we may find it easier to pray to God as Almighty, powerful and strong, but struggle to perceive him as a God of compassion. Certainly, that has been my journey over the years. I knew very early on in my faith journey that God was creator and majestic and worthy of praise; it has been only more recently that I have gained a clear and enduring sense of God as a God of compassion and mercy.

Or it may be that you know God's tenderness and generous care, but struggle to see God as someone who holds the whole world in almighty hands, who is not subject to any other agency or power. Perhaps the message is that however things appear God is still in charge.

I think an episode from the life of the Old Testament prophet Elijah can help. For in 1 Kings 18 and 19 we see both an almighty God and a Father of all mercies. On Mount Carmel we see God Almighty bringing fire onto the sacrifice and leaving the prophets of Baal nowhere to go. But in the wilderness that follows we see the Lord caring for a desperate Elijah through the provision of food, drink and sleep.

I wonder if Elijah gave thanks to an Almighty God and a Father of all mercies.

Looking back at ourselves

If this is the picture of the God who is being thanked, what is the picture of ourselves? One of the toughest things to get used to during those innumerable Zoom meetings during lockdown was looking at a picture of yourself on the screen. It was just not something I was used to and was sometimes a bit of a shock, especially if the screen froze when I was pulling a particularly unattractive face!

Just as I couldn't escape the truth about seeing myself as I really was, the General Thanksgiving starts by describing the person praying – and hopefully that is you and me – in two quite challenging ways.

Unworthy servants

The first thing to notice is that we are described as 'servants'. That is probably not an immediately attractive way of seeing ourselves. It speaks of hierarchy in a world that is much more concerned with visible equality. And it speaks of a lack of agency in a culture where personal autonomy is valued so highly. Surely such a description is unhelpful today?

To be sure, if the only way we describe ourselves is as servants then that will be unhelpful, but I think we need to be careful about writing off such language too early. One reason is that it reminds us what being a follower of Jesus Christ is all about – namely, letting somebody else take the reins. The Apostle Paul describes himself frequently as a 'servant of Jesus Christ' because he wanted to recognize that Jesus was in charge of his life. He was no longer his own man; Jesus was Lord.

And the other value in the language of servant is that we can take joy in whose servant we are. I remember watching the film *Gosford Park* about a shooting weekend in a 1930s country house (it was the forerunner of *Downton Abbey*, if you are interested). One of the oddities that the visiting servants had to get used to was that below stairs they were referred to by the name of their master or mistress. And they took pride (or shame) from how their superior behaved. Now there are lots of things about this we don't want to copy, but it set me thinking how wonderful it is that I can describe myself as a servant of Jesus Christ. He has made me his own and I am his. I don't find being his servant demeaning. It is a great privilege that I am called to love, follow and serve him. I might be Dean of Durham, but more importantly, and wonderfully, I am a servant of Jesus Christ.

The other thing to notice is that we are described as 'unworthy'. This is potentially more of a banana skin than being called a servant. In a world where mental health related to matters of self-esteem is under significant pressure, the question must be raised as to whether giving ourselves the label of 'unworthy' is really going to be helpful.

As someone who has struggled with blaming myself for the sexual abuse I suffered as a child, I know the risks involved here, and certainly I would never want to suggest that calling ourselves 'unworthy' should be the last or only thing we say about ourselves. But when it comes to giving thanks to God, I think it is helpful because it reminds us of how we are made and what we deserve.

The big word is 'anthropology', which means our understanding of what it is to be human. And I think the argument we need to follow goes something like this.

Beautiful and broken

Our culture around us in the West says that we are beautiful as we are, however we define and express ourselves. Social media drives a self-approval culture in which we hear and say to others, 'You are beautiful'. The Christian faith would want to give a hearty endorsement to such a sentiment, albeit for slightly different reasons. The Bible speaks of every one of us being made in the image of God, and so we are beautiful in God's sight as human beings, patterned after our creator God.

However, there is another 'B' that we need to add to the 'beautiful' tag, and that is 'broken'. The Bible speaks of each human being as flawed – by a tendency in each one of us to do things that harm ourselves and others. The technical word for this is 'sin' but this can lead us to think too quickly of specific 'sins' rather than paying attention to the deeper reality that each one of us has got a capacity to make choices that reflect our own wishes rather than those of God who cares for all the world.

John Wyatt, a Christian doctor and theologian, uses the illustration of a wonderful painting that is both exquisite in its beauty but has also been damaged by cracks in both the artwork and the frame.[1] The beauty is still there, but so is the brokenness.

The Bible has some pretty stunning stories of people whose beauty and brokenness was on public display – King David com-

---

[1] Wyatt has used this analogy a number of times at conferences I have attended. For more on his helpful thinking on Christian anthropology, see John Wyatt, 2009, *Matters of Life and Death*, revised edition, Nottingham: IVP.

mitting adultery with Bathsheba is one and the Apostle Peter denying Jesus is another – but for most of us the beauty and the brokenness are much more individual and private.

And yet it is there, however much we want to deny it. One of the things that I find so striking about our contemporary culture in the West is the rise of cancel culture, which effectively labels other people as sinners (it doesn't use that word but that is what is meant) while justifying the people who remain on the good side of the fence. We seem to find emotional energy and moral self-justification in pointing out the errors of others.

But the reality is much more demanding. We are all both beautiful and broken – created in the image of God and stained by the reality of sin. None of us is worthy.

Now those two 'Bs' are not the sum of a biblical anthropology. Our brokenness is not the final word. There is an 'L' to follow which is that we are *loved* (and we will explore that later in the book). But at the outset of this prayer I think it is useful to see ourselves as unworthy for this reason at least – namely, that we don't deserve anything we receive.

Even as I type this, I can feel the hackles rising. 'I worked for that' we say, pointing at the house or job or car that is ours. And that might be true. But on a more fundamental level, as we come before God in prayer we need to recognize that we have no rights or claims for gifts from God's hand. We have no moral perfection that means God owes us anything. All that we have is gift. Getting that straight at the outset is actually the key to the prayer that follows.

Seeing God and ourselves clearly

'Almighty God, Father of all mercies, we thine unworthy servants ... ' How does starting the prayer in this way help us in our giving thanks?

First, it reminds us that all things come from God, who gives out of a Father's love and care. Nothing that we have, for which we will be invited to give thanks, comes from outside God's provision and control. If we have it, it is a gift of God and comes as an expression of his care and compassion towards us. We need to hold together that the earth is the Lord's and everything in it and also that God comes close to us in our need.

Second, it reminds us that none of us has earned our way into God's good books and therefore deserves anything that we have received. We have no claim on the gifts and mercies of God. We do not come holding a contract saying that God owes us this or that; rather, we come with empty hands.

Yet that is an exciting place from which to start. Coming as we do with empty hands, we are in a position to receive. If we come in a spirit of expectation and not entitlement we will be able to see far more as a gift from the Lord's hands. Indeed, if we start from the basis that God is almighty and merciful and we are unworthy, we will be in a position to see all that we have – including life itself – as something for which we can give thanks.

And that includes every breath we take.

3

Everyday Thanks: Learning to Count Our Blessings

*'We ... do give thee most humble and hearty thanks for
all thy goodness and loving-kindness to us and to all men;
We bless thee for our creation, preservation and all the
blessings of this life.'*

I am a morning person, but even for me it is sometimes a struggle.

Part of the service of Morning Prayer, which I pray every morning in the heart of Durham Cathedral, includes these words, 'As we rejoice in the gift of this new day'. Rejoice? Sometimes I feel like doing just that, when I have slept like a log, when the day ahead looks interesting, when the sun is shining through the east window and I can think that the washing I've just hung out is going to dry in no time. Then I find it quite easy to rejoice.

But sometimes those words are a real challenge for me to say and mean. When sleep has been patchy at best, when the inbox and diary are overwhelming, when I know that I am not at my best with myself and others, then it is quite hard to rejoice as a new day dawns.

Yet what helps is that one little word: gift. Each day that dawns is precisely that, a gift, something that I haven't earned and yet which is so, so precious. Simply my existence and capacity to know God's life and love is a privilege that I can't take for granted.

As I have used the General Thanksgiving in my prayers over the years, it has taught me to thank God for the ordinary blessings, such as the gift of a new day. In fact, it has really helped me to find new ways in which I can thank God in the everyday.

They often slip by me, but this prayer helps me notice them and capture them in my heart.

If the first chapter was the story of the 'how' the General Thanksgiving prayer came about and the following chapter was about who is doing the praying and who we are praying to, this chapter gets us going with actually thanking God. It's about God's character towards all, God's creative power in all things and God's generous blessings in all of daily life.

Goodness and loving-kindness

It is said of great sportspeople that 'form is temporary, but class is permanent', and I think the same can be said about character. Character goes to the core of who we are. It drives our behaviour – our words and our actions. If someone's character is humble they don't find it hard to learn from others, however senior they are in an organization. If someone's character is proud, they will get offended by even the smallest slight. The last ten years in the UK have seen the character of political leaders of various hues laid bare through their actions and behaviours; in the long term it has been seen that character matters.

As I have built teams over the years, I have always looked for character above everything else. I am not always that worried if the person has done the job or a similar one before. Skills can be learned but character is permanent.

God's character is that consistent core from which God acts. The God revealed in Scripture is not like one of the ancient deities who could be capricious and vindictive. God's character is reliable and consistent, and it is on two aspects of that character that the General Thanksgiving invites us to focus as we begin to give 'humble and hearty thanks'.

First, we are invited to give thanks to God for God's goodness.

I remember when I was a teenager I used to go over to my grandma's house and read the parish magazine to her. Her eyesight had failed but she wanted to keep up with the news from the church and community. There was one person who used to write quite a few articles from time to time who clearly organized a lot of really worthwhile work from the church into the community. When I got to the end of the article I would read out his name which ended the piece and my grandma would say, 'He's a really *good* man'. It was high praise, as if she recognized that this was a man of unimpeachable integrity and conduct. 'Good' may be a word that has been devalued over the years, but when it comes to character it is one of the best things that can be said about us.

God's goodness is what motivates God's behaviour towards us. The blessings of life (which we will explore in a moment) come not from a God who is trying to drive a bargain with us or curry favour with us, but from a God who is inherently good towards us. As A. W. Tozer writes, 'The goodness of God is that which disposes him to be kind, cordial, benevolent and full of good will toward men ... By his nature he is inclined to bestow blessedness and he takes holy pleasure in the happiness of his people.'[1]

Perhaps you have been in a church where services started with a call and response: 'God is good! All the time! All the time! God is good!' (If you have been in that church, you won't have forgotten it.) We can give thanks to God that there is not a day when God is not good.

Second, we are invited to give thanks to God for God's loving-kindness.

Loving-kindness is one of those old words that I think we should really bring back. It was actually invented by Miles Coverdale, who translated the whole Bible in 1535, and he created it to try and do justice to the Hebrew word *hesed*. In modern Bibles it is translated 'mercy' or 'steadfast love' but I think loving-kindness is so much more evocative and communicates the way in which God acts with generosity, love and kindness towards his children who often deserve something less.

A wonderful place where this is seen is in the story of the Exodus, when the Israelites have worshipped the golden calf in the desert and the original tablets with the Ten Commandments

---

1 A. W. Tozer, 1984, *The Knowledge of the Holy: The Attributes of God, Their Meaning in the Christian Life*, Bromley: STL, p. 82.

have been broken. Two new tablets are made and God speaks directly to Moses:

> The LORD, the LORD,
> a God merciful and gracious,
> slow to anger,
> and abounding in steadfast love and faithfulness,
> keeping steadfast love for the thousandth generation,
> forgiving iniquity and transgression and sin. (Exod. 34.6–7)

In these verses the word *hesed* is used twice, first to describe God's character ('abounding in *hesed*') and second to describe God's action ('keeping *hesed* for the thousandth generation'). God *is* loving-kindness and he *acts* with loving-kindness.

All of which connects back with what we explored in the last chapter when we considered the description of God as the 'Father of all mercies'. God does not treat us as we deserve but with grace (to use the New Testament term) he showers his love on us. How he does this is something we will explore much more in the middle section of this book.

Often when I wake up I switch on the news to find out what is new. I look at my electronic calendar to find out what is in the day ahead. This prayer invites me to focus on what has stayed the same, on what was true when I went to bed and what will be true tomorrow and the day after. God is a God of goodness and loving-kindness. For that I can give humble and hearty thanks.

And here's the wonderful thing. God is not like this only to some people, as if God turned on the charm for them but reverted back to a growl for others. The prayer says that this goodness and loving-kindness is 'to us and all men'. However that sounds to us now, it was a phrase that was meant to include everybody. And nowhere is that seen more clearly than in the two specific reasons which come next in the prayer: our creation and preservation.

Fearfully and wonderfully made

It is quite normal now to see scans of babies in the womb, because they pop up on social media feeds, but I think the first one I ever saw was for my elder son who was born in the mid-2000s. And I remember holding that little bit of computer printout paper and thinking how amazing it was that that little life was being formed in my wife's womb.

But then I remember going further and thinking, 'And I was like that once.' There I was, about to take up the responsibility of being a father, but only 30 years previously I had been formed in my mother's womb. It's not something we think about often, perhaps, our own creation, our own coming into being, but it happened to each one of us.

The writer of Psalm 139 considered this long before scans were available and saw it as a reason to thank God, 'For it was you who formed my inward parts; you knit me together in my mother's womb. I praise you, for I am fearfully and wonderfully made' (Ps. 139.13–14).

Let us note here that the writer of Psalm 139 was not stupid or naive; he knew where babies came from. But he did not see the human agency of new life cancelling out the divine hand. It is a great example for us that a biological account of our creation need not compete with a theological account. The two are complementary.

The General Thanksgiving enables us to thank God for this theological reality. We are invited to bless (i.e. thank) God for our creation. In other words, we are encouraged to thank God that we exist in the first place. 'Thank you, God, for making me, me' is very much the vibe. That is perhaps something we sang about at school (I seem to remember doing so) but it is still true today. Every human being is the result of God's handiwork. And wonderful it is too.

I don't know what you say to yourself when you look in the mirror. It is possible that you think that the person looking back at you is just the most beautiful, perfect specimen of a human being that ever walked this earth. I'm delighted for you. Or, if you're like me, you might notice the bits that are a tad saggy, a little receding and otherwise bordering on suboptimal. But here's the good news: the aim isn't for me to look in the mirror and say 'Well done, Philip, you're wonderful', but rather 'Praise God, I am fearfully and wonderfully made'. Or, in the words of the General Thanksgiving, 'We bless you for our creation.'

While we are on this topic, there is one other thing worth saying. I think our creation continues to be good news as we grow up. As we seek to discover who we are, through adolescence and beyond, we can return to the fact that our bodies are not an accident. We don't have to create ourselves from scratch. We already have a creator who made us.

Carefully preserved

And it doesn't stop there. Everybody can bless God for their creation, but the General Thanksgiving says we can also thank God for our preservation.

Now if we are honest that feels like an odd word to use. Preservation is something that is done to old railways or summer fruit. When I do think of human beings and preservation I think of visiting Lenin's mausoleum in Red Square; the former Soviet leader was certainly beautifully preserved.

So what did Edward Reynolds have in mind when he invited us to bless God for our preservation? I think he was referring to everything that God has given that has enabled us to continue to live our lives. So that includes the food we eat, the water we drink, even the air we breathe. Everything that keeps us going is a gift of God for which we can (and indeed should) return our thanks and praise.

In an episode of *The Simpsons*, Bart is asked to say grace and says these words, 'Dear God, we paid for all this stuff ourselves, so thanks for nothing.' A funny line, but not really what the discipline of saying grace before meals is all about. We say it as a family to build a rhythm of thanksgiving into our lives and to recognize that the food we have may have come from the supermarket but it is ultimately a gift of God. It is part of his daily preservation of us.

And it does include every breath we take. One prayer technique that I have found helpful is to begin by focusing on one's breathing and notice what it feels like. Each breath is a gift of God.

A few winters ago I was walking down a hill in Durham and was too busy looking at the view (of the cathedral as it happens) to see the black ice. Down I went flat on my back and winded myself really badly. And as anyone who has done this knows, you feel for a moment that you can't breathe. You are trying to but nothing is happening. Slowly my breath came back and I staggered home. But one of the things that it taught me is that every breath is a gift of God.

There is a story in the Bible about the prophet Samuel erecting a stone to mark the people of Israel's deliverance from the Philistines. Samuel calls the stone 'Ebenezer' (which means Stone of Help) because, he says, 'Thus far the LORD has helped us' (1 Sam. 7.12). I think the General Thanksgiving's invitation to us to thank God for our preservation is an encouragement for us to do likewise. We are invited to look back on our lives, however bumpy or smooth they have been, and say, 'I am still here because of the Lord's provision and protection.'

Counting our blessings

We're still not quite finished. The prayer has a final stimulus for thanksgiving, which is 'all the blessings of this life'. That sounds fairly comprehensive.

But it is easier said than done. Because in the consumerist West, it is really easy to focus on what we don't have rather than what we do. Adverts work on the basis of getting us to want things: a new coffee machine, a better car, a sunnier holiday. This is amplified by social media feeds that show the highlights of everybody else's lives while we are waiting for the bus in the rain. We are all too conscious of what we are missing out on.

But focusing on 'all the blessings of this life' is an invitation to thank God for what we do have rather than resent what we don't. I can't run as fast as I used to (which was never that fast to be honest) but I thank God that I can still run. I thank God for music which makes me happy, friends who make me laugh, memories that make me cry, hugs that make me feel cared for. We'll think about this more in the conclusion to this book, but a key part of having a thankful heart is noticing the blessings that come our way rather than letting them slip past.

Interestingly, the General Thanksgiving includes space for naming very specific blessings. It includes a phrase in brackets and italics which refers to 'those who desire now to offer up their thanks and praises for thy late mercies vouchsafed unto them'. We can't be sure but I think what Edward Reynolds might have had in mind was a time of informal sharing of news and answers to prayer (which would have happened in the more informal Presbyterian context) which would then be concluded with this prayer. Again, we will think how we use this pattern ourselves later on in the book. For now let's notice the attention that is given to God's blessings being seen in the ordinary things of life.

When blessings are in short supply

There is, however, a nagging question at the back of my mind, and perhaps it is at the back of yours too. How does this language of 'all the blessings of this life' work when life seems to be going really wrong? When a marriage ends, or cancer is diagnosed, or a child goes off the rails, or sin is exposed? Or what about situations where people just have much less than others, and perhaps barely enough to live on?

As we have seen, Edward Reynolds, the author of the General Thanksgiving, was writing at a time when people were having it really hard. Yes, with the restoration of the monarchy there was no war any more, but many of his colleagues were going to lose their jobs in the Church, and people were still living with the horrors of the Civil War fresh in their memory. Yet Reynolds still expected people to be able to count their blessings.

In today's world I don't think counting our blessings is something that is only possible when you get over a certain income level. Indeed, I have noticed that some of the people who have materially least are the most grateful and generous. Conversely, some who have much think they have earned it all, deserve it all and aren't going to give any of it away. Scholars have certainly found more materialistic people report particularly low levels of gratitude.[2] But living a life of thanksgiving is about focusing on what we have received rather than what we haven't.

Thanksgiving for all

Indeed, the point of this part of the prayer is that everyone can take part in this thanksgiving. We can all see that we are not only created but also preserved. Our lives are a gift of God and our daily provision also comes from God's hand. Not only that but all that brings us life and joy comes from a good God who out of his loving-kindness longs to bring happiness to his created children.

What do we need to do to take this step? Fundamentally, we need to believe that we are not on our own. We need to recognize that we are not an accident but are made – by a good and loving God. We need to recognize that for all our agency and our autonomy we are not masters of our universe but that everything we have comes ultimately from the Almighty God and Father of all mercies. That is why our thanks need not only to be hearty (i.e. heartfelt) but also humble.

We noted in the Introduction that scholars suggest that there are two key components to practising gratitude. The first is that we affirm the good things we've received, and the second is that we acknowledge the role other people play in providing our lives with goodness. This opening section of the General Thanksgiving invites us to do the first and in some ways the second, albeit with the vital modification that we are not thanking a person or people but rather the living, loving and providing God.

---

2 Dacher Keltner and Jason Marsh, 2020, 'Can gratitude beat materialism?' in Jeremy Adam Smith, Kira M. Newman, Jason Marsh and Dacher Keltner (eds), *The Gratitude Project: How the Science of Thankfulness Can Rewire Our Brains for Resilience, Optimism and the Greater Good*, Oakland, CA: New Harbinger Publications, p. 182.

GIVING THANKS

We can rejoice in the gift of a new day, not because we are necessarily feeling wonderful or all is right with the world, but because God is good and full of loving-kindness, and we have received the gift of life, in which we are daily sustained and blessed.

And the reasons to give thanks are just about to get a whole lot bigger.

PART 2

Love Beyond Measure: The Heart of Thankfulness

4

Love for the World: Christ's Gift of Redemption

> *'But above all for thine inestimable love in the redemption of the world by our Lord Jesus Christ'*

What's it worth?

Looking at some news reports, it would seem that we love to put a price on things. Stories about famous people – celebrities or politicians – are sprinkled with details about how much things cost: the house they live in, the handbag they are carrying, the shoes they are wearing. Businesses are measured by their turnover – and the salaries of their CEOs. I remember sharing a car journey with a friend who seemed to know the retail price of every car on the road. 'That's £80k of Mercedes right there' he would say, as a car with tinted windows sped past. We can't stop ourselves, apparently, from thinking what things cost.

But there are some things that can't be priced up as easily. A red sunrise in the middle of winter. A walk on a summer's evening. An hour spent at the bedside of a dying relative. These cannot be reduced to numbers or entered on a spreadsheet. You can't put a price on them and it would seem folly even to want to.

Putting a price on love

I think that love is to be found firmly in that latter category. True, there are relationships which give the impression that a financial value can be assessed, as evidenced in a pre-nuptial agreement or a belief that you are worth as much as your latest present; but deep down we know that love doesn't work like that. Love is not a commodity that can be bought or sold. It cannot be transferred by contract from one party to another. Love does not come with a number of noughts on the end. It can't be priced.

And it is perhaps because of this that we are not always good at assessing the true value of love. I like reading the obituaries in the paper (something that my children reckon is a sign of my advancing senility) and am fascinated by the lives that people have led. The reports carry details of posts held, recognition achieved, new ground chartered and legacies left. But to me one of the things that often seems to be missing is any language of love: who they loved and who loved them. Yet in my experience this is what matters most of all. Of far more worth to me than the roles I have undertaken have been the relationships of love that I treasure: in my marriage and with my family and friends.

My wife works with people with life-limiting illnesses and speaks about the clarity that people often have as they approach the end of their lives. And one of the few things that matter is that they can say to those closest to them: 'I love you.'

You can't put a price on love. That is because it is worth so much.

Inestimable love

So it should not be a surprise that love is at the heart of the General Thanksgiving. We've seen so far that Reynolds composed his prayer to lead people on a journey of thanksgiving, and this has involved thanking God for being made, for being sustained and for the blessings of everyday life. But that was just for starters. The main course is announced with a drum roll as the prayer continues, 'But above all ...' Here's the real reason to give thanks to God. Wait for it ...

It is love.

To be accurate it is 'thine inestimable love'. Try saying it out loud. It's quite a mouthful. But it is almost as if Reynolds wants those saying the prayer to linger over it, not to rush past it and miss its significance.

The first thing to note is that this is God's love. The reason to thank God is not for the general gift of love, wonderful though I hope we can all affirm that to be. The prayer invites us to thank God for *his* love, love that we say is 'thine'.

The second thing to note is that this love is inestimable. That's a word we don't hear much these days. It means that it can't be measured. It is simply too large to be calculated. You can't put a number on it. No *Antiques Roadshow* expert would be able to come up with a price – even for insurance purposes.

Thine inestimable love. It is meant to be said slowly. It is meant to sink in. Here we have reached the heart of thankfulness, and we are being invited to ponder not just this love but where it can be seen. The three phrases that follow: a) the inestimable love in the redemption of the world by our Lord Jesus Christ; b) for the means of grace, and c) for the hope of glory provide the answer, and we are going to spend a chapter on each. They take a few seconds to say but they take a lifetime to explore – and enjoy.

First off, we can see this love in the past.

Redeeming redemption

The prayer continues, 'thine inestimable love in the redemption of the world by our Lord Jesus Christ'. But here, I suggest, we hit a problem. If 'inestimable' was hard to get our mouth around, we can at least work out its meaning fairly quickly. But when we get to 'redemption', we find ourselves confronted with a word that we may have heard before but not be quite sure what it means. It is one of those theological words like 'salvation' and 'justification' which we may have heard in readings and sermons but not be crystal clear a) what is in view here, and b) what Jesus has to do with it.

The next section involves us thinking about some fairly big ideas, but I think we will see God's love more clearly as a result.

So what is redemption all about? The first thing to do is go back to the Old Testament (and when we are thinking about ideas in the New Testament the Old Testament is almost always the best place to start). And the key episode to have in view is the story of the Exodus, where at the beginning of the narrative the

Israelites find themselves in captivity under the brutal regime of Pharaoh and are seeking freedom and liberty. And as the story unfolds it tells of the intervention of God to humble Pharaoh and bring the Israelites through the Red Sea and into the Promised Land (albeit going very much the pretty way).

What God did in that story was an act of redemption. It was bringing freedom to a people who were in captivity, and it was achieved not by themselves but by a third party – that is, God. So it was that the episode was later narrated thus:

> It was because the LORD loved you and kept the oath that he swore to your ancestors, that the LORD has brought you out with a mighty hand, and *redeemed you* from the house of slavery, from the hand of Pharaoh king of Egypt. (Deut. 7.8, italics mine)

Redemption is giving people their freedom.

It is also important to note that redemption wasn't just something that God did and left it there. He also called his people to be a redeeming people – that is, bringing freedom to those who are otherwise trapped. That is what many of the laws are about, for example, in Leviticus 25.18–34, and is one of the dynamics at play in the story of Ruth, when she is redeemed from poverty through the actions of Boaz – her kinsman-redeemer. And with his actions she enters into a freedom of her own.

Redemption and the Apostle Paul

Fast forward to the New Testament and we find redemption linked to what Jesus did in dying on the cross. But to understand it we have to look at some assumptions being made which for the modern reader may take some getting our head around.

From the perspective of the authors of the New Testament (principally the Apostle Paul but not just him) there is a problem facing all of humankind. It is not the problem of one tyrannical leader and it is not the problem of just one nation state. It is a problem for all.

In Chapter 2 I spoke about a biblical way of seeing ourselves as both beautiful and broken. Part of that brokenness is that we are all subject to a power that shapes our thinking and acting in unhelpful ways. Paul calls that power 'sin'. For Paul, sin is a much bigger idea than simply the lists of things we might do wrong – lying, stealing, not putting the top back on the tomato ketchup. Sin is a force in the world that means that we put ourselves at the centre of our world rather than the God who made us. It is a sort of gravitational pull which means that we are absorbed with what works for us rather than for others, that we see faults in others but not ourselves, that we are determined to write our own story where we are the hero.

And Paul seems to think that the hold that sin has over humanity is every bit as serious as that which Pharaoh had over the Israelites. This life lived under sin is a form of captivity, and the impact is seen not in poor living or working conditions (like having to make bricks without straw in Exodus 5.7) but in a society where people are living self-centred lives, without reference to God and without the capacity to do much about it. Yes, in the twenty-first-century West these lives are often characterized by great individual freedom, but I think if Paul were to visit us today, he would point out that the areas where we live out our personal freedom – money, sex, power, to name just three – can actually hold us captive. Like all idols, they promise happiness and deliver disappointment.

Interestingly, while some Christians like to personalize this captivity and talk about the power of the devil, Paul doesn't do this very much. He is more likely to talk about the power of death and the law than the power of the devil, but it is sin that gets the largest write-up.

For Paul, however, there is some wonderful news at hand. As he reflects on what took place when Jesus went to the cross, and did so willingly, he understands it as dealing with the problem of sin and its hold over humanity. When he writes that Christ 'gave himself for our sins to set us free from the present evil age' (Gal. 1.4), Paul is articulating the belief that the cross put an end to the power of sin in the world. When Jesus offered his life on the cross, he gained the freedom of all those who would trust in him.

In other words, it was an act of redemption.

So it is that Paul can write of Jesus, 'In him we have redemption through his blood' (Eph. 1.7). So it is that he could say to believers in Corinth, 'You were bought with a price' (1 Cor. 6.20) while reminding them that Christ Jesus is, for them, 'Righteousness and sanctification and redemption' (1 Cor. 1.30).

A freedom event

An illustration might help. It comes from *Les Misérables* by Victor Hugo, a spellbinding novel even before it was turned into a world-famous musical. Jean Valjean, who will in time become the story's hero, starts in troubled straits. He has left prison on parole and stays a night at the house of a bishop, Monseigneur Bienvenu. Unable to withstand temptation, he steals the bishop's silver cutlery and makes a bid for freedom. He is soon caught and returned to stand before the bishop, fearing judgement and a return to prison. But in an act of generosity and grace, the bishop tells the police that he gave Valjean the silver and wants him to have the silver candlesticks as well. He tells him to go on his way and finishes with these words: 'Jean Valjean, my brother, you no longer belong to what is evil but to what is good. I have bought your soul to give it from black thoughts and the spirit of perdition, and I give it to God.'[1] This was an act of redemption, and the rest of the novel is about Valjean's attempt to live redeeming acts of his own.

Now that is not a perfect illustration by any means. But hopefully it conveys something of the sense of liberty and freedom that is tied up in the word 'redemption' and is an important part of the good news of Jesus Christ.

We can often associate the death of Jesus with securing our forgiveness. 'Christ died for our sins' is what the early Christians were taught (1 Cor. 15.3) and it has found its way into our songs and liturgies and prayers. And that is certainly true. But the cross is such a wonderful, epoch-changing event that it cannot be

---

1 Victor Hugo, 1980, *Les Misérables*, translated by Norman Denny, London: Penguin Books, p. 111.

reduced to one dimension of meaning. And the New Testament is clear that along with being declared not guilty through the cross (what is technically called justification) we are also set free from all that made us captive (and that is redemption). In other words, we are freed not only from the penalty of sin but also from the power of sin. We are free to serve God. Sin does not and will not have the final word.

And it is about to get even better.

For God so loved the world

Because there is one final thing I want us to notice about this phrase in the prayer which is taking us to the heart of thankfulness. And that is the words that come in after 'the redemption': 'of the world'.

It would have been quite easy (and perhaps more expected) for Reynolds to write 'thine inestimable love in our redemption through the Lord Jesus Christ'. But he doesn't. He uses the words 'redemption of the world'. This phrase is not drawn directly from Scripture, but it is found in one of the prayers Thomas Cranmer wrote for the Book of Common Prayer in 1552, the exhortation before Holy Communion. Reynolds seized on this phrase and used it in his prayer, and we need to consider what he might have had in mind.

We can't be sure but I suspect there may be two things at play in Reynolds using this phrase. The first is that Reynolds is stressing that redemption is available to all and not just some. Reynolds was only too well aware of the contemporary theological controversies of the day, one of which was whether Jesus had died for all, or for just the elect – that is, those whom God had chosen for eternal life. The Westminster Confession said that by the decree of God, 'Some men and angels are predestinated unto everlasting life, and others foreordained to everlasting death.'[2] Now Edward Reynolds came from this theological stable but I

---

[2] Westminster Assembly (1643–52), 1646, *The Humble Advice of the Assembly of Divines, Now by Authority of Parliament Sitting at Westminster, Concerning Part of a Confession of Faith Presented by them*

can't help hearing in this phrase an emphasis that this redemption is for all, and not just some. It is for the whole world.

And there is good scriptural backing for this view. What is perhaps the most famous verse in the Bible – John 3.16 – states very clearly: 'For God so loved the world that he gave his only Son, so that everyone who believes in him may not perish but may have eternal life.' This redemption, this freedom from living with sin in charge, and freedom to live with Jesus as Lord, this is for everybody.

And there is a further implication of the reference to the world that I can't help but think of, and that is this: when Reynolds mentions the redemption of the world as a reason for thanksgiving, I think he is inviting us to look beyond our individual experiences of redemption to the bigger picture.

One of the charges levelled at the theological emphases of the Reformation is that they stressed rather too much the individual nature of salvation and left wider society out of it. The emphasis was on an individual getting right with God, and if the evil world was doomed to perish so be it. This is one reading of John Bunyan's classic *A Pilgrim's Progress*, written a couple of decades after this prayer was written.

But in introducing the phrase 'redemption of the world' Reynolds is inviting us to lift our eyes beyond our own stories to those of people around us, the society and world in which we live. What does it mean to say that it is not just individuals who can be set free, but also the whole world? Are we being given a glimpse here of a whole society being redeemed – from the power of sin into a whole community living for God?

The great social reformers of the nineteenth century, such as Elizabeth Fry, Josephine Butler and Lord Shaftesbury, were people convinced of the need for personal redemption but also for a redemption that impacted society. I wonder if 'redemption of the world' was a phrase that spoke to them.

I think of this as the coming kingdom of God which Jesus spoke about so much in his ministry. Here we see individual lives being redeemed not in order to be put on a salvation lifeboat

---

Lately to Both Houses of Parliament, London: Printed for the Company of Stationers, pp. 8–9.

and watch the rest of the ship go down but to be part of a wider redemption as Jesus the king establishes his kingdom.

Beautiful, broken, loved

I have written already of two things to remember about who we are as human beings: we are both beautiful and broken. Here's the third and most important one: we are loved.

We are loved by our creator God, not grudgingly or stingily but generously and lavishly. He gave his Son for us, to die not only for our sins but to secure our freedom. The New Testament tries to describe this love in lots of ways: 'riches of his grace that he lavished on us' is how Paul puts it in Ephesians 1.7–8. Later in the same letter he talks about 'the boundless riches of Christ' (Eph. 3.8). The General Thanksgiving simply says: 'inestimable love'.

This inestimable love comes not in the form of a warm smile from the other side of the room but a God who comes down to earth, taking the very worst that human beings can do to one another and using it for God. This is love in action. 'In this is love,' the Apostle John says, 'not that we loved God but that he loved us and sent his Son to be the atoning sacrifice for our sins' (1 John 4.10).

And this love poured out on the cross achieved something lasting: not simply the forgiveness of sins but a new way of living, a way centred not on ourselves and under the siren-voice of sin but rather free to love God and live for God. Sin is not in charge. We have been bought with a price. We belong to God. And so we can be part of his redeeming work in the world.

Remembering redemption

I want to take us to another scene from *Les Misérables*, this time right at the end of the novel. Jean Valjean is nearing the end of his life, and the scene is his living-room, to which his bed has been moved. And on the mantelpiece, we are told, are the bishop's candlesticks in their usual place. He has kept these signs of his redemption all his life, and they have formed the focus for his life lived in the service of God. They have helped him remember his redemption.

I find myself doing something similar most mornings. I make a cup of tea and go back to bed and listen to a prayer meditation while holding a wooden cross firmly in my hand. Simply holding it (sometimes very tightly) reminds me of the most important thing in my life, more important than any of the jobs I have to do each day. It reminds me I am loved and redeemed. Loved by God in Jesus Christ. Loved so much that I am under new ownership (that's how I think of redemption). I don't have to live for myself or be pulled by the gravitational pull of sin. I can live for the Son of God 'who loved me and gave himself for me' (Gal. 2.20). And I can be part of his redeeming work in the world.

Writing on living a life of thankfulness, Jeremy Adam Smith talks about how 'gratitude thrives on specificity'.[3] In other words, to use his examples, we don't just thank our spouse generally for their love but mention the pancakes they make, the massages they give and the hugs they offer.

The General Thanksgiving invites us to do the same with God. We are not just thanking God for a character of loving-kindness (although in the prayer we did just that) but for a specific act of love, that act of Jesus dying on the cross for the redemption of the world.

Whatever else is going on in our lives, we can be thankful for God's inestimable love in the redemption of the world by our Lord Jesus Christ. You can't put a price on that.

Inestimable love poured out in the past. Now for love poured out in the present.

---

3 Jeremy Adam Smith, 2020, 'How to cultivate gratitude in yourself' in Jeremy Adam Smith, Kira M. Newman, Jason Marsh and Dacher Keltner (eds), *The Gratitude Project: How the Science of Thankfulness Can Rewire Our Brains for Resilience, Optimism and the Greater Good*, Oakland, CA: New Harbinger Publications, p. 78.

5

Love for Today: The Means of Grace

'for the means of grace'

Anyone who has worked with or looked after teenagers knows that access to wi-fi is as important – perhaps more so – as fresh air.

I remember travelling with my family across mainland Europe as part of an interrailing trip. We arrived in Berlin, found the flat we were renting and were met by the host. She spent a short time greeting us and telling us where things were, and then mentioned wi-fi. 'Don't worry,' one of my sons said, 'we're already on it.' In the couple of minutes she had been speaking, he had located the handbook to the flat, found the wi-fi code and logged on. Now he could breathe.

This is an understandable reaction. So much of a teenager's social life is accessed online that access to wi-fi is important for maintaining a sense of connection to friends and what they share together. Without wi-fi a teenager can start to feel very lonely.

This chapter is – wait for it – about a sort of spiritual wi-fi, the way we stay connected to God's irestimable love. It is about something called the means of grace, a term that needs some explanation and exploration in order for us to see how it can be part of our giving thanks today.

A surprising move

It is actually quite surprising that the phrase is in the prayer at all, and the fact that it is is a further hint that Bishop Edward Reynolds and the prayer he wrote are rather more innovative than we might at first imagine.

Because it would have been entirely possible to stop the sentence with the reference to redemption, in which case the prayer would have read: 'above all for thine inestimable love in the redemption of the world by our Lord Jesus Christ. And we beseech thee, give us that due sense of all thy mercies ... ' Given that Jesus' death on the cross represented the supreme example of God's inestimable love, it would have made sense to focus on this act in the past as the chief reason to give thanks to God. But Reynolds does not do that. He continues the sentence with phrases which move from a focus on the past to a focus on the present ('the means of grace') and the future ('the hope of glory') as well.

However, at this point we have to address an important question. How do these three phrases relate to one another? Are they three distinct reasons to give thanks: a) inestimable love and redemption, b) the means of grace, c) the hope of glory, or is there a thread that holds them together?

While grammatically they can be seen as distinct – the repeated 'for' in the General Thanksgiving acts as a sort of bullet point creating a list – I think that theologically we should see them together. Specifically, I would argue that God's inestimable love should not be seen as applying simply to the first phrase alone. Yes, that is where the grammar takes us, but we must, I think, let that note of love continue to ring and sound through the next two phrases as well. Inestimable love in redemption, yes, but love in the means of grace and the hope of glory too.

So as we explore the means of grace, we should be looking out for how they connect us to God's inestimable love.

The meaning of 'the means of grace'

But before we do that, we need to identify what exactly is in view when the prayer talks about the 'means of grace'. It is a term that has been extensively used by churches across the theological spectrum, but when Reynolds was writing his prayer it doesn't seem to have been in common currency in England. Certainly it is not used anywhere else in the Book of Common Prayer, something that can come as a surprise to people who think it is a dyed-in-the-wool Anglican term.

In fact, I think the most likely place Reynolds got it from (although we can't be sure) was from his Presbyterian days under the Commonwealth. The Westminster Shorter Catechism, produced in 1647 by the Westminster Assembly of which Reynolds was a part, included this question and answer:

> Q: What are the outward and ordinary means whereby Christ communicates to us the benefits of redemption?
> A: The outward and ordinary means whereby Christ communicates to us the benefits of redemption are his ordinances, especially the word, sacraments, and prayer; all which are made effectual to the elect for salvation.[1]

The means of grace are thus those things through which God works in the present to bring the benefits of redemption into the believer's life. They are channels through which God's grace – that is, his free gift – is able to be received. To put it in General Thanksgiving terms, if the redemption of the world is the act that reveals God's inestimable love, the means of grace are how believers receive that inestimable love into their hearts.

The Apostle Paul wrote to the church in Rome, 'God's love has been poured into our hearts through the Holy Spirit that has been given to us' (Rom. 5.5). This is not simply a one-off event, as if redemption were simply a ticket to be acquired. Rather, the Spirit-filled means of grace enable us to receive God's love in the here and now, day by day.

So here is the key question for us to ask if we are going to pray this prayer with meaning. How do the means of grace help us connect with God's love? As we look at the means of grace with which Reynolds would have been familiar – Scriptures, sacraments (especially Holy Communion) and prayer – I think we will find further reasons for giving thanks, and avoid some spiritual cul-de-sacs on the way.

---

1 The Westminster Standard, n.d., 'Shorter Catechism', https://thewestminsterstandard.org/westminster-shorter-catechism, accessed 25.04.2025.

Prayer

I don't tend to see the devil behind every broken lightbulb, but, in the tradition of C. S. Lewis's classic *The Screwtape Letters*, I do think one of Satan's minor victories is getting so many Christians to feel guilty about prayer. People speak to me about not doing it enough (or at all) or not doing it right. There are lots of 'shoulds' and 'oughts' and preachers don't necessarily help the situation by putting prayer at the top of the list of 'things you really must do this week'.

But what does prayer look like when we see it as a means of grace? How would we feel about prayer if it was not something we felt we were responsible for doing regularly, but rather something that was available to us 24/7 as a way of receiving the inestimable love of God?

I've always struggled with one particular bit of Jesus' teaching on prayer. It's the language of 'reward' from the Sermon on the Mount (you can read the passage in Matthew 6.5–6). Jesus criticizes the hypocrites for making a big show of praying in public. He says, 'Truly I tell you, they have received their reward.' And then Jesus says, 'But whenever you pray, go into your room and shut the door and pray to your Father who is in secret; and your Father who sees in secret will reward you.'

At first sight it appears that Jesus is saying that if we pray in the right way we will earn a reward, perhaps the answer to prayer that we are hoping for. But what if the reward were not as instrumental as our requests being granted? What if the reward was more fundamental than that? If a retreat to a secret place indicates a desire to encounter God in a profound way, might that not be the reward Jesus is referring to?

I wonder if the greatest reward of prayer might be to know the amazing love of Christ which Paul prayed about in Ephesians 3.18–19. There he prayed that the believers 'may have the power to comprehend, with all the saints, what is the breadth and length and height and depth, and to know the love of Christ that surpasses knowledge'. That sounds to me like inestimable love, and it is prayer that is the key to knowing it.

I take part in lots of prayer at Durham Cathedral. I say lots of words written by others – some from the Scriptures, others in set liturgies – and I write a fair few prayers of my own. But in all the services that take place, I have found that for me there is something deeper going on, a desire to be attentive to the love of God revealed in Jesus Christ. In other words, for all the speaking that goes on, what is more important is what I am receiving. It is almost as if the speaking opens up a channel for the really important part, which is receiving the love of God afresh.

I use the Pray As You Go app in the mornings, a resource from the Jesuits in the Ignatian tradition. Its strapline is, 'Become aware of God's gaze of love upon you.' I think it is a great way to approach prayer: that fundamentally it is about receiving God's love in the everyday, and that is the basis for everything else.

One of the great gifts of the Orthodox tradition to the wider Church has been the Jesus Prayer, which goes back to at least the fourth century and was popularized in the nineteenth century in the book *The Way of a Pilgrim*.[2] The following words are designed to be repeated numerous times, perhaps at the start of a prayer time or as the entire focus for prayer itself: 'Lord Jesus Christ, Son of God, have mercy on me, a sinner.'

Former Bishop of Coventry Simon Barrington-Ward has written beautifully on what it means to use this prayer daily.[3] If I had to summarize its impact on me, it is that it switches me from request mode to receive mode. In other words, it orientates me away from what I need to what God wants to give me, which is an assurance of his love. I don't pray for mercy wondering whether it will appear. I know it will because of Jesus' love poured out on the cross. But it gives me the chance to receive it afresh.

I do still ask for things, particularly for other people on my heart. But those requests are rooted in a deeper prayer of receiving God's love.

Prayer is a real means of grace.

---

2 Andrew Louth (ed.), 2017, *The Way of a Pilgrim: Candid Tales of a Wanderer to His Spiritual Father*, London: Penguin Classics.

3 Simon Barrington-Ward, 2007, *The Jesus Prayer*, Oxford: The Bible Reading Fellowship.

Bible

If there is another thing Christians can feel guilty about, it is not reading the Bible enough. In fact, we seem to spend more time feeling guilty than we do reading it. Many Christians approach Bible reading like preparing for an exam; we think we should try and read more and more so that we can remember as much as possible and know the difference between the Urim and Thummim, and which minor prophet comes before Malachi.

Now I love the Scriptures. I spent six years doing a PhD on 1 and 2 Corinthians. I taught New Testament to ministers-in-training. But I don't find reading the Bible on my own always very easy. I knew lots of people who read the Bible in a year, so after about 15 years of being ordained I thought I would try it. If I am honest, it was a real slog and I came away thinking 'never again'. Even to this day there are lots of details about the Bible I just can't remember. If it was an exam, I don't think I would do that well.

But what does the Bible look like when we see it as a means of grace? How might we see it if we approached reading the Scriptures less as something we do to find out more about God, and more as something through which God shows his love to us?

The prophet Jeremiah, going through one of his not uncommon periods of gloomy introspection, remembers a time when God's word was exactly this means of grace, 'Your words were found, and I ate them, and your words became to me a joy and the delight of my heart' (Jer. 15.16).

I mentioned the Ignatian tradition in talking about prayer, and its approach to the Bible has been similarly helpful for me. This approach is rooted in a belief that the Holy Spirit has specific things to show us as we encounter God's word, and engaging with God's word therefore involves being attentive to what God wants to show us. This involves a fair degree of waiting, often coming back to a passage more than once, a good amount of imagination and a belief that God is alive and active and wants to reveal himself to us.

I often find myself saying as I hear God's word – either in services at the Cathedral or at home on my own – 'What do you want me to receive today, Lord?' In effect, how do you want to use this portion of Scripture as a means of grace? To put it simply, I am in receive mode.

Morning Prayer on Tuesdays has been one such moment for me. The Church of England's Daily Worship material involves us saying some of Psalm 103 together and it includes these words from verses 1–5:

> Bless the LORD, O my soul, and all that is within me, bless his holy name.
> Bless the LORD, O my soul, and forget not all his benefits;
> Who forgives all your sins and heals all your infirmities;
> Who redeems your life from the Pit and crowns you with faithful love and compassion;
> Who satisfies you with good things, so that your youth is renewed like an eagle's.

Those words are a means of grace to me. They put me into receive mode and I receive afresh God's tenderness and kindness to me in the everyday.

To be clear, I am not saying there is not a place for regular reading of Scripture to discover more about God's ways and character. It is just that if we turn Bible reading into a chore we need to get right, we are missing the point. The Scriptures are a means of grace, an invitation to know more of God's inestimable love.

Holy Communion

And so to the sacraments, which for the Reformers would have meant the sacraments of Holy Communion and baptism. Given that baptism is something that only happens to us once (although it is wonderful to be part of a church where baptisms are a regular occurrence), I am going to focus on something which we do much more often – namely, partake in Holy Communion.

Now you might know it under another name: the Lord's Supper, the Eucharist, the Mass, and the different names point to diverse understandings of what is going on in this most central of services in the life of the Christian Church. I am not going to pronounce on the rights and wrongs of anything, but I do want to explore an approach (a classically Anglican one as it happens) which helps me see the sacrament as a means of grace.

The Reformation – which took place in the century before Reynolds wrote his prayer – was a time of sharp division in understandings of the Lord's Supper. The traditional view of the Church was that the bread and wine became Christ's body and blood and were offered as a sacrifice on behalf of the Church, a remaking of Christ's sacrifice on the cross. Some Reformers, in rejecting that, went to the other extreme and saw it as purely a remembering of what Jesus did, a calling to mind of what he had done on Golgotha.

Thomas Cranmer took a middle way, a way that is still to be seen in the Book of Common Prayer today. For him the bread and wine remained just that – bread and wine – but it also became spiritual food for the believers who came to the Lord's table in penitence and faith. Such believers received Christ's body and blood spiritually and were nourished and fed as they ate and drank.

In other words, the focus is not what is going on at the table but rather what is going on – what is being received – in the heart of the believer. That is why Cranmer's approach is often called 'Receptionism'. The focus is on what is being received.

One of the prayers to be said after receiving communion expresses this really well. I quote the opening part of it in full, while noting that the language is quite complex.

> ALMIGHTY and ever-living God, we most heartily thank thee,
> for that thou dost vouchsafe to feed us,
> who have duly received these holy mysteries,
> with the spiritual food of the most precious Body and Blood
> of thy Son our Saviour Jesus Christ;
> and dost assure us thereby
> of thy favour and goodness towards us;
> and that we are very members incorporate

in the mystical body of thy Son,
which is the blessed company of all faithful people;
and are also heirs through hope of thy everlasting kingdom,
by the merits of the most precious death and passion of thy
dear Son.[4]

Basically the message is this: in receiving spiritually the body and blood of Christ, we are being assured that we are loved – with an inestimable love.

We can thank God for Holy Communion as a means of grace. As we come with open hands, we can come hopefully, expecting that we will receive Christ into our hearts and thereby assurance of his inestimable love.

I can think of times when I have been struggling with my faith – feeling far from God, feeling anxious about the future, feeling convicted about my own sin – and receiving the sacrament into my hands and my body has been a wonderful means of grace. I am in receive mode – and have received afresh God's inestimable love.

God's love today

Here's one of the best bits of news about Christian faith: God's love was not just for yesterday.

It is a source of much sadness to me when I encounter Christians who are thankful that God's love was poured out for them in the past, but in the present day feel guilty about everything else. 'I'm not a very good Christian' is the earworm. 'I don't read my Bible enough, I don't pray enough, last time I received communion I was worrying if I had locked the door when I left for church.'

But the means of grace (and we've only looked at three in this chapter, although there are more) are not there to make us feel guilty. There are gifts to help us know each day that God's inestimable love was not just poured out on the cross but can be poured into our hearts each day.

---

4 Book of Common Prayer, Cambridge University Press edition, pp. 258–9.

This is the spiritual wi-fi we all need. And it is there 24/7.

I wonder what it means for you to thank God for the means of grace. Does it help you see the Bible, prayer and Holy Communion in a new light? Does it help you see them not as chore but as gift?

We can thank God for the means of grace through which we know God's inestimable love in Christ. Love for today. And, as we will see next, love for ever as well.

6

Love Forever: The Hope of Glory

'and for the hope of glory'

Are things getting better?

A quarter of the way through the twenty-first century, things are not turning out as we thought, at least as far as the West is concerned. The new millennium saw democratic progress in many corners of the world, with a concomitant belief that the world was coming together, albeit with a few rogue outlier states. In the UK this was the era of New Labour, of material steps forward in terms of education, child poverty and healthcare outcomes. Things were getting better.

Twenty-five years on it is difficult to maintain that same sense of optimism. The tectonic plates of global politics have moved substantially, and there are threats to both economic stability and world peace that are real and concerning. Populist leaders are on the rise, promising a brighter future for nations but with apparently less concern for the rights of an individual. Birth rates in the West are declining at a sharp rate; it seems that bringing new lives into the world is not as popular as it once was. Home ownership, that bellwether of economic aspiration, is fading as a realistic hope for many. Mental health challenges, especially among the young, are on the rise.

Of course, there's always next season.

That's the sports fan's response. Rather than look to the long-term horizon, the football, cricket or rugby supporter (and I must confess to being all three) sets their sights on the next 12 months. A couple of new signings, fewer dodgy referee/umpire decisions and a fair wind behind us and next season could really see us improve. We might make the top half of the table. The play-offs aren't out of the question.

I've been in that place. With three sports and teams on the go there is usually room for a glimmer of hope somewhere. But as any sports fan will tell you, 'It's the hope that kills you.' Hope for a sports fan usually falls far short.

Hoping against hope

So what are our grounds for hope? If the idea that the world is getting better is now under serious question, on what basis can we look to the future, if not with optimism, then perhaps with confidence?

Because the reality is that we need hope. Ted Lasso, the football manager in the hit comedy of the same name, rails against his team's sense of despair. 'It's the lack of hope that kills you', he says to them before a crucial game.

But what is a hope worthy of its name? And how can this hope offer us a further reason to give thanks?

We have seen that at the heart of the General Thanksgiving is a focus on God's inestimable love, and we have noted that this love has been expressed not only in the past (in Christ offering redemption for the world through his death on the cross) but also in the present through the means of grace, by which we can access God's love in the everyday. However, the prayer invites us to see this wonderful love in a future perspective as well, as it invites us to bless God for 'the hope of glory'. But what is this hope of glory? And how does it help us to know God's inestimable love – and thus give thanks – in our daily lives?

The weight of glory

Glory is a very rich theme in the Bible, not least in the Old Testament where God's glory is understood to reside in the Jerusalem Temple. But when it comes to the hope of glory, there are at least two phrases in Paul's letters that can help us think about what glory looks like from a future perspective. These are Romans 5.2, 'we boast in our hope of sharing the glory of God', and also 2 Corinthians 4.17, 'For this slight momentary affliction is preparing us for an eternal weight of glory beyond all measure'.

Paul is clearly looking beyond the grave here, to the reality of the resurrection life which he so powerfully depicts in 1 Corinthians 15 and which is described elsewhere in the New Testament. The Apostle Peter refers to this when he writes of 'an inheritance that is imperishable, undefiled, and unfading, kept in heaven for you, who are being protected by the power of God through faith for a salvation ready to be revealed in the last time' (1 Pet. 1.4–5). The book of Revelation paints a picture of a new creation where 'Death will be no more; mourning and crying and pain will be no more, for the first things have passed away' (Rev. 21.4).

So far, so hopeful, but where does glory fit in?

C. S. Lewis, in a famous sermon on Paul's reference to the 'weight of glory' in 2 Corinthians 4.17 (a sermon delivered, it should be noted, in the darkest days of World War Two), writes of the weight of glory having two dimensions to it. The first dimension of glory referred to divine approval for lives lived in the service of God. Lewis said:

> The promise of glory is the promise, almost incredible and only possible by the work of Christ, that some of us, that any of us who really chooses, ... shall please God ... To please God ... to be a real ingredient in divine happiness ... to be loved by God, not merely pitied, but delighted in as an artist delights in his work, or a father in a son – it seems impossible, a weight or burden of glory which our thoughts can hardly sustain. But so it is.[1]

The hope of glory is that we will be welcomed and loved by God as those who have pleased him. Lewis concludes, 'The door on which we have been knocking all our lives will be open at last.'[2]

---

1 C. S. Lewis, 1942, *The Weight of Glory*, London: SPCK, p. 7.
2 Lewis, *The Weight of Glory*, p. 8.

And the second aspect of glory that Lewis notes is about enjoying the light and beauty of God face to face. Lewis writes powerfully of how the beauty of creation points to a deeper beauty beyond:

> Nature is mortal; we shall outlive her. When all the suns and nebulae have passed away, each one of you will still be alive. Nature is only the image, the symbol; but it is the symbol Scripture invites me to use. We are summoned to pass in through Nature, beyond her, into that splendour which she fitfully reflects.[3]

So what does this hope of glory look like in terms of knowing God's inestimable love? We can see it in this way. This love was seen in the past when Christ poured out his love on the cross; it is known in the present through God using the means of grace to feed and fill us with such love; and it will be encountered in the future when we come face to face with the one who is and always will be love. The hope of glory is nothing less than being enveloped in the inestimable love of God. It is what awaits every person who has looked to Christ and placed their trust in him.

But we might be left with a nagging question at this point. Is the hope of glory really something that far off? Is hope just about when we die, or the Lord comes again, or can it impact us rather sooner than that?

Hope starts now

Here I think we see again Edward Reynolds's brilliance in writing the prayer as he did, for in using that exact phrase 'the hope of glory' he points us to a place that invites us to see hope in an excitingly different way.

Because the fact is that there is only one place in the whole of the New Testament where the words 'hope of glory' are used, and that is in Paul's letter to the Colossians, where the apostle wrote of the saints thus: 'To them God chose to make known

---

3 Lewis, *The Weight of Glory*, p. 9.

how great among the Gentiles are the riches of the glory of this mystery, which is Christ in you, the hope of glory' (Col. 1.27).

Christ in you, the hope of glory. That phrase opens up a new way of seeing the hope of glory – namely, as something that is not simply about when we die, but rather something that starts now as the physically absent Jesus is spiritually real to us by the power of the Holy Spirit.

In other words, the hope of glory is not a completely different category of experience that we can only look forward to but with little understanding of what it involves. We see through the glass darkly, but we do see. We know Christ with us and in us now, as the Holy Spirit works in the sacraments, in Scripture and in prayer, and that gives us a foretaste of what is to come.

Let us take Holy Communion as an example, and a prayer that Thomas Cranmer wrote for believers to pray before they came to the Lord's table. It starts with the words, 'We do not presume to come this thy table, merciful Lord, trusting in our own righteousness', and so is called the Prayer of Humble Access. And it ends with these words:

> Grant us therefore, gracious Lord, so to eat the flesh of thy dear Son Jesus Christ and to drink his blood, that our sinful bodies may be made clean by his body, and our souls washed through his most precious blood, *and that we may evermore dwell in him, and he in us.* (italics mine)

'Evermore dwell in him and he in us.' This is a phrase not just about the present but the future. It is recognition that Christ's presence with and in us now has a continuity with what the future holds. Life in the new creation will be a fulfilment of the life with Christ we know now. It is striking that when the Apostle Peter at the start of his first letter talks of future hope (as we read earlier), he roots it in present experience: 'Although you have not seen him, you love him; and even though you do not see him now, you believe in him and rejoice with an indescribable and glorious joy' (1 Pet. 1.8).

In Holy Communion we receive Christ in us in such a lasting way that we can taste the glory of when we see him face to face.

It is not the main course, not even the starter. It is one of those little dishes they give you in a posh restaurant to get the taste buds going. *Amuse bouche* is the technical name I understand. It assures you that the best is yet to come.

Because Christ in us is the hope of glory. And we have that hope in us now.

Hope, life and death

So how does this hope of glory help us to live thankfully in a world that seems increasingly uncertain?

Put simply, the hope of glory invites us to lift our eyes beyond the present. I think we can be a little bashful in speaking about the hope of glory, but this prayer helps us think about it in exactly the right way.

The hope of glory is not about some distant celestial liturgical love-in, where harp-playing is not only requested but required. It is about the fulfilment of something that starts now and is part of the good news for now. The means of grace are such that we can know Christ and his love with us and in us, and the hope of glory is that we will see that Christ face to face. This does mean that we shift our focus from the present, but it does remind us that the present is not all there is, and the future is not in the hands of the politicians, it is in the hands of God.

Every morning in Durham Cathedral I say Morning Prayer in the Feretory, the shrine of St Cuthbert, where that great saint has rested for over 1,000 years and been a focus for pilgrimage and prayer. Cuthbert was a saint who lived in very uncertain times, in seventh-century Northumbria, in a largely pagan society where Christianity was just beginning to take root. There were threats from home and overseas and life was rarely stable.

And yet Cuthbert knew God's inestimable love – not least through the means of grace. His commitment to the life of prayer was exacting and challenging, but it is clear that he encountered Christ fully in the midst of it. He loved the Scriptures and particularly John's Gospel, and although a copy of that book, which is called the Cuthbert Gospel (and incidentally has the oldest known Western bookbinding to survive), dates from shortly after his death, it was placed in his tomb precisely because of his affection for God's word. And at Durham Cathedral we still have the portable altar that he would take with him on his travels as he celebrated Mass in the villages where he had taught and evangelized.

But if Cuthbert knew about the means of grace, he also knew about the hope of glory. And the evidence for that comes not from his life at all, but from his death, or rather his dying, about which we know quite a bit.

Now that itself might strike us as slightly unusual. Modern biographers – and writers of obituaries for that matter – usually say little about the manner of someone's death. But Bede, writing the life of Cuthbert just over 40 years later, gives quite a detailed account of his death, using a first-hand account from Herefrith, Abbot of Lindisfarne at the time of Bede.

> When it was time for the night-time prayers, Cuthbert received the sacraments from me, and fortified himself for his departure, which he knew was to be soon, with the Body and Blood of our Lord. Lifting up his eyes and hands to heaven, his soul, hungry for heavenly praise, parted to the joys of the kingdom of heaven.[4]

We might ask why Bede includes this story. The answer I suggest is that for Bede the manner of Cuthbert's dying said everything about his living – and the hope that connected the two.

I think it is like this. We think today that life is what matters. It is about activity, achievement and status. It is about getting on and making a mark, whereas death is the extinguishing of all that. Nothing happens. It is the end. So life and death are complete opposites, the one to be celebrated and the other to be avoided (and thus ignored).

But for Cuthbert life and death were joined together by a great commonality and that was God. God wasn't a hobby for Cuthbert, a lifestyle choice. God was the very centre of his being. And

---

4 Simon Webb (ed.), 2016, *Bede's Life of St Cuthbert*, in a Modern English Version, Durham: Langley Press, ch. 39.

just stopping breathing wasn't going to change that. In life he served God and sought God. In death he placed himself in the hands of the God who raised Jesus from the dead. Indeed, as Sister Benedicta Ward has shown, his death was patterned on the self-giving of Jesus himself.[5]

For Cuthbert, the gap between living and dying wasn't the great chasm it appeared. God would be his centre in both contexts because death was not the end. His example reminds me of the words of the Apostle Paul who says to the Philippians that he can't decide between living and dying, 'For to me, living is Christ and dying is gain' (Phil. 1.21).

Living backwards

Everything in our society today says that we should live life forwards, acquiring an education, a career, a relationship, a mortgage, a pension, a bucket list, and lots and lots of stuff. The hope of glory as seen in the death – or rather the dying – of Cuthbert challenges us to look at our lives from a different perspective. The challenge might be something like this: how would it be to live our lives backwards, to imagine how we would like to face death and shape all our other choices accordingly? Or to put it another way, what might it look like to start by thanking God for the hope of glory and work backwards from that?

Because here is the exciting thing. For Cuthbert, living life backwards didn't lead to inactivity or depression; it led to risk-taking, fruitful service and infectious, transparent, lasting joy. He was always going to be with Christ, so even in unsettled times he did not have to hold on to that which he could not keep. The hope of glory didn't mean he avoided reality. It meant that he entered into reality seeking the redemption of the world but knowing it wasn't all down to him.

The North American thinker Zena Hitz has written a penetrating examination of contemporary culture in her recent book *A Philosopher Looks at the Religious Life*. Her analysis is that

---

[5] Benedicta Ward, 1992, *The Spirituality of Saint Cuthbert*, Oxford: Fairacres Publications, pp. 11–14.

we avoid confronting death because death challenges our desire for getting more stuff. She writes, 'Death makes acquisition futile; it reduces us to the poverty of birth.'[6] Yet for her, facing up to the reality of death can actually be a profoundly fruitful stimulus to finding a life of true meaning, because it shows how the religious life of faith and prayer offers something much more real and lasting than is often supposed.

It is called the hope of glory. Christ's love in us. Starting today.

I don't think any contemporary approaches to gratitude involve thinking about death. But it faces us all. One of the things that the General Thanksgiving does so well is root our gratitude not simply in the past and the present but the future as well – because whatever the future holds, it will not separate us from God's love in Jesus Christ (Rom. 8.38–39). And that is something to be really thankful for.

Love yesterday, love today, love forever

Edward Reynolds's wonderful prayer has shown that at the heart of thanksgiving is God's love, God's inestimable love. This love was poured out on the cross for the redemption of the world, it is poured into our hearts through the means of grace, and it will be poured over us as we see God face to face. This is love in the past, love in the present and love in the future. The common feature is Christ, who died on the cross, who by the Holy Spirit comes to us in the means of grace and who is the hope of glory.

I wonder which aspect of this love has touched us most over the last three chapters. Has there been something that has come to us as new or unfamiliar? Or if it has felt something we were already aware of, how has it felt to reflect on it at a slightly slower pace? I said earlier that simply saying 'thine inestimable love' is an invitation to slow down, and I hope we have taken our time over the phrases that followed. Because however much we know of God's love, there is always more to discover.

---

6 Zena Hitz, 2023, *A Philosopher Looks at the Religious Life*, Cambridge: Cambridge University Press, p. 26.

But what next? We've seen how this love changed someone like Cuthbert, but we've got more to find out about how thanking God isn't something we just pray.

It is something we do.

And that walk will take us into the very life of God.

PART 3

Living Gratefully:
The Practice of a Thankful Life

7

Letting It Sink In: A Thankful Heart

'And we beseech thee, give us that due sense of all thy mercies, that our hearts may be unfeignedly thankful'

I think it will be clear by now: I love a thank you letter. It warms the cockles of my heart when someone has been to stay or come for dinner and then writes to say thank you. I don't need the thanks, but it brings me to joy to read what that stay or supper meant to that person, how they received it as a gift and how it blessed them.

A thank you letter is a response to something that has been received. It recognizes the reality of gift and emotional bonds that are created in giving and receiving. My kids might tell me I am hopelessly old-fashioned but I think there is considerable mileage in paying attention to the dynamics of gift and response. And as we saw in the Introduction, gratitude is a growth industry.

The General Thanksgiving is – no surprise here – not a thank you letter but a thank you prayer. It is about both gifts received and a response offered. The first half of the prayer has been exploring the gifts, that is, the blessings that are received. These are both the general blessings of life (creation, preservation and so on) and the specific blessings of Christ – namely, God's inestimable love poured out in redemption, the means of grace and the hope of glory. This opening part of the prayer has been like climbing a mountain and we have now got to the top, with a commanding view of God's wonderful love poured out in the past, the present and the future.

But the path down the mountain awaits, and we are going to need to pay close attention to what a faithful path looks like. There are three stages to be navigated, all relating to aspects of ourselves: we are called to have thankful hearts, thankful lips and thankful lives. The first and third get most of the airtime in the prayer, and so they are going to be our focus for the next two chapters.

So this chapter is about having thankful hearts. And, as we will see, it is our hearts that shape everything else.

At the heart of it all

But first we have to tackle another word that I suspect may be unfamiliar. The prayer asks for hearts that are 'unfeignedly thankful'. 'Unfeignedly' is probably not part of our everyday lexicon, but it means genuine or not fake. So hearts that are unfeignedly thankful are hearts that are thankful not out of duty or to tick a box but out of a deep sense of what has been received.

But we need to ask, why all this attention on our hearts in the first place? What is it about our hearts that means that they are the first stop in the thanksgiving journey?

We can easily think that our hearts are purely about our emotions. They are what we put on a social media post when we like what we see. They are what are plastered over Valentine's Day cards. When our relationship comes to an end it is our hearts that are said to be broken.

But in the ancient world, the world of the Bible, a world that heavily influenced the thinking of theologians such as Thomas Cranmer and Edward Reynolds, the heart is understood to do much more heavy lifting than simply feeling a range of emotions. The heart is used figuratively as the place of our priorities and desires, from which flow our decisions and our actions. In the rational post-Enlightenment West we think it is the mind that determines what we do; for many generations before, it was the heart.

Some examples from the Bible might illustrate this point:

- It was Pharaoh's hard heart that led him to refuse the Israelites the freedom they so desperately wanted.
- It was the Israelites' rebellious hearts that led them to wander in the wilderness.

- It was David's heart that needed addressing after he had committed adultery with Bathsheba.
- It was Solomon's heart that was commended by God when he asked for wisdom rather than riches.

When Jesus said 'it is from within, from the human heart, that evil intentions come' (Mark 7.21) he was certainly challenging the tradition of the Pharisees, who seemed keener on external rather than internal purity, but he wasn't saying anything that hadn't been pointed to before. And at another point he confirmed the centrality of the heart when he said 'out of the abundance of the heart the mouth speaks' (Matt. 12.34).

When it comes to the centre of our decisions and actions, it all flows from the heart.

Adam Peaty, the Olympic swimmer, seemed to get this when he spoke after the 100-metre butterfly in the Paris Games of 2024, when he was beaten to gold by two-hundredths of a second. 'I'm a very religious man, and I asked God to show my heart, and this is my heart. I couldn't have done any more.' He knew that his actions told only part of the story. It was his heart that mattered.

Our hearts are what really matter. If giving thanks is going to happen, and happen unfeignedly, it needs to start within our own hearts.

A heart problem

However, as the biblical examples quoted above suggest, our hearts are complex and there is little evidence to suggest that they have changed fundamentally since biblical times. And when it comes to nurturing hearts of gratitude there are two problems that can occur, both mentioned in the Bible.

First, there is the problem of a *proud heart*.

Jesus tells the story of a Pharisee who went up to the temple to pray. Standing by himself he prayed in the following terms: 'God, I thank you that I am not like other people: thieves, rogues, adulterers, or even like this tax-collector. I fast twice a week; I give a tenth of all my income' (Luke 18.11–12).

Here is a man looking down on others, listing his religious works and taking his place on the moral high ground. Here is a man all too conscious of what he regards as his own achievements. Here is a man with a proud heart. The prince of Tyre clearly sees himself in a similar position of strength, only this time it's political and the prophet Ezekiel speaks the Lord's judgement against him: 'Because your heart is proud and you have said, "I am a god; I sit in the seat of the gods, in the heart of the seas", yet you are but a mortal, and no god' (Ezek. 28.2).

A proud heart is not purely the preserve of religious and political leaders. We are all encouraged to point to our achievements and what we have done. I found my record of achievement from secondary school a while back: a cracking blue plastic folder with some yellowing music certificates and mark sheets from the odd public speaking competition or two. But look at any CV or LinkedIn profile and there is a dizzying list of workplace achievements that we can point to and say, 'I did that.' I am no exception: when I applied for the role of Dean of Durham, I had to set down all I had done in my roles to date.

There is nothing wrong with this, other than it runs the risk of making us think that we have done all this ourselves and on our own. As we list our achievements we can focus on our own efforts and agency, and pride flows very naturally from that. And a proud heart stops us seeing all that we have as a gift.

And it can happen to anybody. I remember once visiting a centre of theological research where everyone was researching some aspect of the Bible. I was visiting the head of the centre and made a passing comment about the spirit of collegiality that I thought must exist. He replied that this was far from always being the case and explained to me the egos and pride that he had to manage as part of his role. So much so, he said, that he wanted to put up a Scripture verse over the entry to the library. It would be from 1 Corinthians 4.7 and addressed to each academic: 'What do you have that you did not receive?'

Their proud hearts were getting in the way of receiving everything as gift.

The second problem is that of a stubborn heart. It was again the prophet Ezekiel who received this judgement from the Lord, but this time it was directed not at a pagan prince but rather at the people of God themselves. He is told, 'But the house of Israel will not listen to you, for they are not willing to listen to me; because all the house of Israel have a hard forehead and a stubborn heart' (Ezek. 3.7). They are locked into a way of thinking, and will not deviate from it.

I think the risk of our hearts becoming stubborn is when we are locked into an outlook that says we do not have enough and that we need more. Western materialism has been successfully exported across the world, and every human being is now classified as a consumer, whether we are in America, India or China. Apart from this being a miserable way of describing human beings, it also means that we are bombarded with messages telling us that we don't have enough. We are programmed not to be satisfied. I get messages from my mobile provider telling me how much better my broadband could be. I need a phone which is newer, better, faster, smaller.

I remember talking to someone in a rich corner of the Home Counties. They lived in a house worth well over a million pounds and had an index-linked pension that allowed them to take cruises and enjoy other luxuries. But they were comparing themselves to some of the bigger houses and cars that they saw on their trips out. And I've always remembered the punchline they gave: 'Talk about how the other half live.'

The other half! This person was in the richest 10%, probably 5%, in the country, but they were focusing on what they didn't have rather than what they did. Their heart couldn't see it another way.

As long as our hearts are stubborn and we are focusing on what we don't have, rather than what we do, we will struggle to be thankful.

Humble and open hearts

So what sort of hearts might be ready for thankfulness?

First, I think hearts that are humble.

Back to the story of the Pharisee and the other character that

Jesus describes. A tax-collector this time, who stands far off, beats his breast and does not even look up to heaven. His words are these: 'God, be merciful to me, a sinner!' (Luke 18.13). Jesus says that he went home right with God, because 'all who humble themselves will be exalted' (Luke 18.14).

Note that this is not forced humility or faux humility, as in the wonderful Uriah Heep in Charles Dickens's *David Copperfield* who says, 'I am well aware that I am the umblest person going.' Yet this humility masks a villainous heart, whose actions form the background to the second half of the novel.

No, a right humility comes from an honest assessment of who we are, something we saw earlier. We are beautiful, yes, and we are broken. We are made in the image of God and we have sinned against God. There is a reason why before we come to the Lord's table for Holy Communion we call to mind and repent of our sins, in words Edward Reynolds would have used from the Prayer of Humble Access. 'We are not worthy so much as to gather up the crumbs from under thy table ... ' That should burst our pride.

But above all, our humility should flow from a recognition that we did not make ourselves, that we are created beings and all we have is a gift from our Creator. Yes, we may have done things, but who gave us the gifts with which to do them? Yes, I can write quite quickly but who gave me my mind (and formed my fingers for that matter)? Yes, I can run 5k but who put the strength in my legs?

A humble heart focuses less on what we have achieved and more on what we have received.

Second, I think we can nurture hearts that are *open*.

One of Jesus' most famous parables is that of the sower. It is there in Mark 4.1–9 but is told in Matthew and Luke as well. The thing is, though, that it is not really about a sower at all; it is much more about the soil. Because there are four types of soil described, and only one of them produces the right context in which God's growth can occur.

The monks who lived and wrote in the desert from the third century used to speak of 'working the soil of the heart', and I think that is a helpful image for us here as we think about nurturing hearts that are open and ready to receive from God. Like soil that has been weeded and tilled and prepared for sowing, through humility and prayer our hearts can become open to receive what God has for us.

Our garden in Durham has a wonderful set of bulbs that come up from early on in the year. First there are the snowdrops, then the crocuses, then the daffodils, then the bluebells. Each day when I go out of the front door I am invited to ask the question: what can I see today? I am required to be attentive and notice.

Now I have to confess that I find this hard. Friends or colleagues will know that I like to be organized and planned. I work off to-do lists and diary engagements. My role involves munching through emails and chairing meetings, which involve me exercising quite a bit of agency and leadership. The challenge for me is having an open heart that is ready to receive something from God, something I might not be expecting or might not have planned for, but which the Lord wants to give me.

That due sense of all thy mercies

Back to the General Thanksgiving because it reminds us that while humble and open hearts may help us be thankful, what will really fire our thankfulness is a recognition of all that God has given us or, as Reynolds calls it, 'a due sense of all thy mercies'.

Earlier on in the book we noted the habits of thankfulness that are recommended by experts in this field today. They involve noticing and recording what we have received, and the part others have played in our receiving them. Having a due sense of all God's mercies involves us doing the same and attributing to God our thanks for these different sorts of blessings.

As we look back over the prayer, I think there are three types of mercies we can remind ourselves of here.

First, there are creation mercies. These are the blessings of the created order in which we live – be it dramatic vistas or a crocus appearing through the snow. But they are also our creation, our own bodies, the fact that we are alive at all. Every time I go for a run I try and remember to thank God that I can run at all. Thank you Lord for making me, me.

Second, there are everyday mercies. This is the language of 'preservation' that we noted earlier. We can notice and thank God for the food on the table, the shelter over our heads, the breath in our lungs. A friend of mine taught us to pray to and thank God for 'journey mercies'. Everyday mercies are still a reason to thank God.

Third, there are eternity mercies. I am not sure this is quite the right phrase, but what I am trying to capture is the 'above all' section of the General Thanksgiving and we have already established that 'inestimable love' doesn't exactly trip off the tongue. But these are the mercies of just that love being poured out, poured into and poured over us in Christ. Inestimable love yesterday, today and forever. Love to fill our hearts to the brim, like the jars were filled at a wedding in Cana, to overflow in thanksgiving to God.

We are invited to ask God to show us these mercies afresh, so that our hearts will be joyfully, naturally and unfeignedly thankful.

We may be asking, yes, but how do we do this practically? One of the tools can be to capture our reasons for thankfulness in a prayer journal and note down each day or week what we want to give thanks for. Another might be a form of *examen* prayer, when towards the end of the day we reflect on the day that is past and ask God to show us where God's life was present and why we might want to give thanks. A further tool might be to use the General Thanksgiving and pause at the end of the sentence 'and all the blessings of this life' and use the silence to offer God our thanks. What is good to do is to ask God to help us to give thanks, to show us the mercies we are being invited to notice.

When the going is tough

All of the above may sound good when things are going well, but what about when the dishwasher breaks, the dog is sick on the floor and you've put a black pen in with the whites wash (I am asking for a friend here). Or more seriously, what about when real problems hit and there is the reality of anxiety, illness, death and grief?

The first thing to say is that a thankful heart does not deny the reality of pain. The General Thanksgiving is not the only prayer we are encouraged to pray. In fact, just before its place in the Book of Common Prayer are prayers to be said in time of dearth and famine, in time of war and tumults, and time of 'any common plague or sickness'. The book of Psalms is all the permission we need to cry out to God in our need. I have done this many times, for myself and others. In other words, thanksgiving is not the only thing we do.

But the other thing to suggest is that a thankful heart seeks mercies in the pain. Yes, we can cry out in our need, yes, we ask God why this is happening to us, but if our hearts are humble and open we can also seek mercies in some surprising places.

I remember waiting to give evidence in the trial of the priest who sexually abused me as a boy. I had given some of my evidence and there was a lunchtime break before the court came back. Giving evidence had been a gruelling experience so far, and I wanted to be anywhere else in the world than that waiting room at that time. I was alone in the room except for a volunteer from the Witness Support Service. She simply sat and held my hand as I cried and cried. And yet to this day if you asked me if I had ever seen an angel it was that woman whose name I never knew and who I never saw again. It was as if Jesus was sitting next to me. I came away from that day with lots of emotions, but one of them was thanks.

Hearts unfeignedly thankful

Before I took on my current role I had a full-body medical. It came back with the surprising news that my metabolic age was rather younger than my physical age ('Yes, but what about your hair age?', was my children's crushing response).

But the key question we are all invited to ask is not a physical one at all: what is the state of our hearts? Are they proud and stubborn, confident in our own achievements and tied to a narrative of wanting more? Or are they humble and open, willing to recognize all that we have as gift and ready to receive blessings as from the hand of God? Do we have a living sense of all God's mercies or is that something we only did some time ago?

Because it is from our hearts that our actions will flow. Thankful hearts lead to thankful lives.

8

Giving Up Ourselves: Leading Thankful Lives

*'and that we shew forth thy praise, not only with our lips,
but in our lives; by giving up ourselves to thy service,
and by walking before thee in holiness and righteousness
all our days'*

Ask most volunteer sports coaches out on playing fields at weekends what motivates them, and they will say that they want to give something back. Often they have had a great time playing sport in their youth and they want to give an opportunity to the next generation. They feel that their sport has given them so much (fun, friendship, experiences) and so they want to give something back.

Thankfulness for the past shapes service in the future.

We have reached the point in the General Thanksgiving when we think about our own lives and our own response. So far the prayer has invited us to speak out praise to God for mercies received and ask that our response will start with thankful hearts. But that is not the end of the journey, for the prayer invites us to ask that we may show God's praise 'not only with our lips but in our lives'.

But what will this look like? What stops the General Thanksgiving being something that we not only say (with our lips) but actually do (in our lives)? What difference does giving thanks actually make?

Here once again Reynolds gives us much to ponder. As the prayer unfolds we are going to see that a thankful life involves both a decision and a lifestyle. Both are rather counter-cultural, but both are good news.

Giving up ourselves

If you go to the Forum in the centre of Rome today, you can still see wonderful temples dating back to the first century. They are extraordinary constructions dedicated to different gods and emperors. Just walking past them you get a sense of the awe such buildings were designed to arouse.

What is harder to imagine, however, is the noise and the smell that would have been present when life and worship in the Forum were in full swing. Because these temples were not places for personal devotion and reflection. They were where ritual sacrifices took place and that involved food being offered but also animals being sacrificed in order to elicit the gods' help and favour with regard to a certain preferred outcome.

I well remember being in central Europe on a church trip and hearing a pig being slaughtered in the next-door garden – it was not a sound I will forget. Ancient Rome would have had that sound – and in the hot summer months, the smell – daily.

Writing to the Christians in Rome in the middle of the first century (when this cultic behaviour was in full swing in the city) the Apostle Paul employs the language of sacrifice as he begins to bring his great missive into land, 'I appeal to you therefore, brothers and sisters, by the mercies of God, to present your bodies as a living sacrifice, holy and acceptable to God, which is your spiritual worship' (Rom. 12.1).

Here Paul is subverting the prevailing understanding of sacrifice in three important ways. First, he says that the believers in Rome should offer up not food or animals but themselves. 'Present your bodies', he says. Second, he says that these sacrifices (of themselves) should be living and not dead. Third, he says this should be done in response to God's mercies, not to earn them. This last point needs a little drawing out because the phrase 'by the mercies of God' is capable of different readings. But an alternative translation is 'in view of God's mercies', and this is one because of the 'therefore' at the start of the sentence and the positioning of this request in chapter 12, after Paul has spent 11 chapters expounding the gift of God in Christ.

Instead of offering dead animals to please God, Paul says, you should offer your own self as a living sacrifice to thank God. It is the other way round entirely.

This is exactly the tenor of what the General Thanksgiving is trying to express when it describes what the thankful life looks like. Reynolds's use of 'giving up ourselves' has strong echoes of Paul's words in Romans 12. It reflects both a decision and a response on the part of the believer to what God has done in Christ.

Ever since the earliest days of the Church this is what a response to Christ has been understood to involve. We have some good evidence from the third and fourth centuries that the early liturgy of baptism involved a person facing west and renouncing the devil and all his works and then turning to face east and making a three-fold commitment to Christ in response to questions from the priest or bishop. Nowadays this is what this commitment sounds like in the Church of England's liturgy:

Do you turn to Christ as Saviour?
I turn to Christ.

Do you submit to Christ as Lord?
I submit to Christ.

Do you come to Christ, the way, the truth and the life?
I come to Christ.[1]

There is no getting away from the fact that this is strong stuff. This is a decision and commitment to come under Christ's lordship and authority, to follow him and walk in his ways.

The Methodist Covenant prayer, which is often said at the beginning of a calendar year, puts it even more simply when it starts with the following words 'I am no longer my own but yours.'[2]

This is what giving up ourselves looks like.

---

1 Church of England, 2000, *Common Worship: Services and Prayers for the Church of England*, London: Church House Publishing, p. 353.

2 Methodist Church, 1999, *The Methodist Worship Book*, Peterborough: Methodist Publishing House, p. 290.

To thy service

But how can this be good news? Surely yielding to someone else's authority is the opposite of what human flourishing is meant to look like? Life is the quest for increasing levels of personal autonomy so that our sense of agency increases and we are dependent on, and answerable to, ever fewer people. We explored this briefly earlier, but surely the language of servanthood and service has had its day?

The important thing is whose service we are entering. When we are invited to give up ourselves it is 'to thy service' – that is, the service of God in Christ. We are not serving a capricious master who wants to exploit us. We are serving the one who is love and wants to give us life.

This is what lies behind Jesus' words to his disciples just after Peter has confessed Jesus for who he is – namely, the Christ. 'If any want to become my followers', Jesus says, 'let them deny themselves and take up their cross and follow me.' This is basically what 'giving up ourselves to thy service' points to. But note how Jesus carries on, 'For those who want to save their life will lose it, and those who lose their life for my sake, and for the sake of the gospel, will save it' (Mark 8.34–35).

When we give up ourselves to the service of Christ, we are offered life in return. A life filled with love. A life filled with meaning. A life filled with God's presence. A life of being useful to, and used by, God. This is not necessarily an easy life but it is life lived in the love of God.

'Giving up ourselves to thy service' is not something we need to say grudgingly. We can say it with joy because in so acting we enter the life that Jesus promised, life in all its fullness.

There is a wonderful prayer we use regularly at Durham Cathedral, from the service of Mattins, or Morning Prayer, from the Book of Common Prayer. It starts with these words, 'O God who art the author of peace and lover of concord, in knowledge of whom standeth our eternal life, whose service is perfect freedom'.

Whose service is perfect freedom. This is one of the glorious paradoxes of the Christian faith, that in giving up ourselves to the service of Christ we find the freedom that comes from life in him. I am not free to do exactly as I want, but that route never promised life anyway, even if initially it seemed to do just that. But I am free to explore and enjoy the life that Christ offers.

When I became Dean of Durham, I was given a decent-sized key called a 'church key'. It doesn't sound like much, but effectively it is a master key that opens most of the doors in the Cathedral. It means I have the freedom of the place. So over the last couple of years I have been taking that key and exploring the extraordinary building that is Durham Cathedral. I can see a door and think: what is behind that? And I can explore.

Life in Christ offers this freedom. Life with Christ is spacious and inviting, with more to discover and more to experience. I have walked with Christ for over 30 years and there has always been more to discover.

Remembering our baptism

We did not reflect much on baptism as a means of grace in Chapter 6, but it makes sense to do it here. Because while baptism is a one-off event (and it may be one we do not remember if we were baptized as children), it is something so fundamental to our identity that we should reflect on it often.

At Durham Cathedral we get the chance to do this quite a bit. At a number of points in the Christian year we fill a bucket with water and sprinkle the congregation with it as a reminder of their baptism (it is a bit more decorous than it sounds, but only a bit). And alongside the sprinkling we ask people to remember and reaffirm the vows made at baptism (and which they affirmed in their confirmation). It is a way of inviting us all to remember regularly the key decision we have made and the identity that defines us: with a due sense of all God's mercies, we have given ourselves up to the Lord's service.

I am no longer my own but yours.

Walking before thee

My childhood involved visiting a large number of National Trust properties. If I am honest they all blur into one in the end. But one of the things I recall was the different stairs for the owners and the servants. The owners would have a grand escalier and the servants would have narrow stairs taking them round different parts of the house. There were also often hidden doors so that servants didn't have to use the public corridors. It was all engineered to ensure servants could not be seen. They did their thing and then went away.

This is what is still associated with servants. The 2022 film *Triangle of Sadness* is set on a luxury yacht where the servants are told to get out of the way of guests. They are meant to be invisible.

The General Thanksgiving may use the language of servants, but it envisages servants of God in a much more relational way. Because as well as 'giving up ourselves to thy service' it also describes us as 'walking before thee'. The language here has echoes in Psalm 116.9, 'I walk before the LORD in the land of the living', and also Solomon's words in his prayer of dedication in 2 Chronicles 6.14 when he talks of God's servants 'who walk before you with all their heart'.

The picture is this. As servants of God we do not live our lives downstairs, hidden from view and only appearing before the master when summoned or when we have a job to do. Everything we do, everything we offer back to God, is done in God's presence.

Now that could feel scary, as if in a Big Brother way God is monitoring our behaviour and waiting for us to trip up. But there is a much more positive approach we can take. Ask any child whose parent has come to watch them in a school play or concert: how did they feel when they knew they were being watched? Most would say it felt wonderful to be noticed.

In serving God we are invited to walk before the Lord.

In holiness and righteousness

Yet the question still poses itself: what does this walk look like? The General Thanksgiving uses a phrase from another Book of Common Prayer prayer, the Benedictus, the song of Zechariah from Luke 1.68–79 (in fact, Reynolds uses a few phrases from vv. 74–75). The old translation has 'that we being delivered from the hands of our enemies might serve him without fear, in holiness and righteousness all the days of our life'.

Yet if this passage shows us where Reynolds got his words from, another passage sheds more light on what it means to pray them. When the Apostle Paul wrote to the church in Ephesus, he structured his letter very carefully, both to explain the different facets of God's good news in Christ (chapters 1—3) and also to explore what it is to live a life in response (chapters 4—6). As part of the latter half, he says, 'You were taught to put away your former way of life ... and to clothe yourselves with the new self, created according to the likeness of God in true righteousness and holiness' (Eph. 4.22, 24).

The principle here is clear: the Christian lifestyle is to be patterned on the character of God. In other words, we are to reflect God in how we live. So just as God is holy, distinctive in purity, so we are called to holiness. Just as God is a God of justice, so we are called to pursue righteousness.

It is both interesting and sad to note that some Christians feel more attracted to living out one characteristic of God more than the other. Some stress the importance of personal holiness, of being pure and set apart from the world, whereas others emphasize the value of social justice, of righteousness on a community level. But the General Thanksgiving doesn't split the two, Paul doesn't, Jesus didn't and neither did the prophets. When Amos called out the leaders of his day it was for both sexual immorality and not looking after the poor (Amos 2.6–7).

So what does walking before God in holiness and righteousness look like? Well, it means praising and pleasing God on the one hand in how we use our bodies, what we look at online, how we speak and what we wear, and on the other hand in how we use our money, how we give to and care for those in need, how we look after creation, how we fight for truth and accountability.

Now as I write this I am only too conscious of my sins of commission and omission: that which I have done and that which I have failed to do. But the answer to this is not to hide downstairs and hope the master never calls. This isn't a game of Snakes and Ladders where every sin involves me sliding down the biggest snake to the beginning. I am walking before a Lord to whom I belong and who loves me and cares for me. My calling is under the loving gaze of God who enables me to pick myself up, receive the Lord's love and forgiveness and start walking again.

But here's the other thing. We can't go around pretending holiness and righteousness are not important. They are. They are how we reflect God's character in the world. They are what God is seeking from us, not in order that we will be loved but in response to the love we have received.

All our days

On 5 February 2022 the late Queen Elizabeth wrote a letter marking the 70th anniversary of her accession to the throne, which was to occur the following day. In it she referred to a pledge she gave on her 21st birthday in 1947, that 'My whole life, whether it be long or short, shall be devoted to your service.' It was a pledge she renewed 75 years later and although the letter was typewritten, there were three words handwritten at the end, in somewhat spidery writing, understandably so for a woman who was 95. The three words were: 'Your Servant, Elizabeth'.

One of the most extraordinary things about Queen Elizabeth's reign was the consistency with which she lived out that pledge. She did not waver from seeing her reign as one of service, and this enabled her to navigate times of great change and challenge to both the monarchy itself and the UK and Commonwealth. When so much was up for grabs, she understood her vocation. And she became one of the most respected people in the world.

By using the phrase 'all our days' the General Thanksgiving not only draws on the words from Luke, it also invites the person praying to lift their eyes beyond the present to the years ahead. It is an invitation to affirm that our commitment to walk before the Lord is not a time-limited offer but rather a direction we intend to walk for the rest of our lives. This is who we are. This is what we are called to be and do.

Life-time commitments are in short supply today. We change employers, insurance providers, even banks. A dog is for life, we are told, but that is the dog's life and not the entirety of ours. Marriage involves life-long promises, but some commentators are questioning whether that is actually realistic any more.

The General Thanksgiving is an invitation to reaffirm our commitment to walk with the Lord until we see him face to face. Every time we say the prayer we are invited to look to the future and affirm that, whatever it holds (and who would write the script for the next 25 years?), we will walk in the same direction.

All our days.

A life of thanks

One of the most helpful things about the General Thanksgiving is that it enables us to get things the right way round.

It is so easy to think of the religious life as something offered to God by way of an imposition, as an attempt to please God and make God like us or love us. The General Thanksgiving is clear that this isn't the case. The religious life in Christ is not a 'please' life. It is a 'thank you' life. Now that does not make it any less demanding, but it does mean that there is no room for being afraid, for we are walking in the way of inestimable love.

And that walk will take us into the very life of God.

9

It's Not About Us:
All for the Glory of God

'through Jesus Christ our Lord, to whom with thee and the Holy Ghost be all honour and glory, world without end. Amen.'

When I lead Evensong at Durham Cathedral I sit opposite the tomb of Bishop Thomas Hatfield, who was Bishop of Durham from 1345 to 1381. Restored in the early twentieth century, it is full of colour, the design of blue and gold attracting the eye amid all the Norman stone of the Quire. But it is what is above the tomb that really takes the breath away, for there is the Cathedra, the seat or throne of the Bishop of Durham, which Hatfield designed and then had completed in 1381, the year of his death.

It is an imposing construction: 16 large steps lead up to the throne which is almost three metres above the ground. Legend has it that Bishop Hatfield wanted it to be the highest throne in Christendom so sent two monks to Rome to measure the Pope's throne there, so that Hatfield could build his higher! Whatever the truth of that story, it is clear that the throne was built to inspire awe on the part of the observer. The Bishop of Durham, looking down from on high on his clergy and people, was to be seen as someone worthy of glory and honour.

It probably wasn't entirely uncontroversial when it was built (although Bishop Hatfield doesn't come across to me as someone who welcomed critical feedback) but what is certain today is that the throne is quite a complex piece of liturgical furniture. Both within and beyond the Church we are increasingly aware of the risks of inappropriate levels of deference. We are sadly all too familiar with stories of abuse perpetrated by those in positions of unquestioned power. Such an environment leads to the question: has the giving of honour had its day?

Yet it is with giving glory and honour that the General Thanksgiving concludes, and if we are to pray the prayer unfeignedly (having learned this word we may as well use it) then we need to consider carefully what it means. Why is it appropriate to end the prayer in this way 'through Jesus Christ our Lord, to whom with thee and the Holy Ghost be all honour and glory, world without end. Amen'? And what does it mean for us to pray it?

Pulling back the curtain

To help us think about this I want to take us to the final book of the Bible, the book of Revelation. Many of us may think that we are due a bit of a health warning here, because however familiar we may or may not be with Revelation, we are probably aware of the powerful imagery and strange language that the book contains. Whore of Babylon, bowls of wrath, four horsemen of the Apocalypse – it doesn't present as a comforting read.

There's no denying the challenge in reading many parts of Revelation, but one thing that is often underplayed is the way that the book is about the present as much as it is about the future. This is certainly true of the letters to the seven churches in chapters 2 and 3, but I think it is also the case with the picture of heavenly worship in chapters 4 and 5.

We can often think that heaven is located sometime in the future, but as Tom Wright has helpfully shown, 'Heaven is the extra dimension, the God-dimension of our present reality.'[1] So we can see Revelation 4 and 5 as the curtain being pulled back to give a glimpse into the worship that is occurring even now.

We are in a throne room, and the scene is depicted as one of awe and wonder: jewels glisten and lightning flashes. We are not being presented with a photo; this is a feeling of what it is like to be in the throne room of heaven. There is one seated on the throne, around whom are four living creatures and 24

---

[1] N. T. Wright, 1994, *Following Jesus: Biblical Reflections on Discipleship*, London: SPCK, p. 86.

elders, falling down in worship. And they sing, 'You are worthy, our Lord and God, to receive glory and honour and power, for you created all things, and by your will they existed and were created' (Rev. 4.11).

The first reason why God is given glory and honour is because of God's creation. The elders are voicing the belief seen across Scripture that God is the source of all life, the creator of all things. To look at creation, therefore, is to be provoked to give glory to God.

'The heavens are telling the glory of God', says the Psalmist, 'and the firmament proclaims his handiwork' (Ps. 19.1). When we see a beautiful sunset, or a mountain range, or a delicate flower, we are not primarily being invited to analyse its construction, but rather to let our sense of awe flow naturally into praise of our Creator God. That is not in any way to denigrate the scientific method that seeks to understand the creative process, but it is to let our hearts take us naturally from considering creation to giving honour to the Creator.

There is a wonderful book by retired professor Brian Roberts called *Building Durham Cathedral*.[2] It explores the different (and often pioneering) techniques employed by the builders nine centuries ago to construct this wonderful place of worship. It is a fascinating account of columns and piers, transepts and vaulting, and includes some tantalizing insights into the phases in which the building was constructed.

But the fact that most people don't know any of this doesn't hinder in any way the most usual response people make when they see Durham Cathedral for the first time, from whatever angle. And that is, 'Wow'. Before their minds analyse, their hearts sing.

I remember a walk I undertook with two friends in the Palestine West Bank about a decade ago. We journeyed south from Nablus, staying overnight with Palestinian families en route. As we came to Taybeh, a Christian village north of Jerusalem, we stopped at the top of a hill to look at the view south, and indeed all around. It had been a journey of both considerable

---

2 Brian K. Roberts, 2023, *Building Durham Cathedral*, Cheltenham: The History Press.

beauty and much pain, as we walked through the rich red soil of the olive groves and heard the suffering of those who lived in occupied land. And yet looking at the view I felt I couldn't stop myself. I found myself singing at the top of my voice the hymn 'O Lord my God when I in awesome wonder'. My friends joined in as we thanked God for his glory seen in all creation.

Glory in the cross

The scene in Revelation moves on and we move with it. In the throne room there is tension in the air, as a sealed scroll is seen and the question posed of who is worthy to open it. No one is found worthy to open the scroll, and the writer begins to cry with grief.

We don't have to work out what exactly this scroll represents, for the focus moves to the one who is found to be worthy to open it, and it is the reason for this that should occupy our attention. The writer sees 'a Lamb standing as if it had been slaughtered', and it is this Lamb who takes the scroll (Rev. 5.6–7). First of all the living creatures and the elders, and then thousands of angels sing a new song of praise:

> You are worthy to take the scroll and to open its seals, for you were slaughtered and by your blood you ransomed for God saints from every tribe and language and people and nation; you made them to be a kingdom and priests serving our God, and they will reign on earth. (Rev. 5.9–10)

> Worthy is the Lamb that was slaughtered to receive power and wealth and wisdom and might and honour and glory and blessing! (Rev. 5.12)

Again, you don't have to understand everything that is going on to get a sense of the overall picture. Here is Jesus, the Lamb of God, being worshipped precisely because of his death, his sacrifice. This Jesus receives the honour and the glory not despite being slain, but because he was slain.

In chapter 4 God is worthy of glory and honour because of creation. In chapter 5 God is worthy of glory and honour because of the cross.

It is an astounding claim to be making at that time. Here is someone who had been submitted to the humiliation of a Roman execution being called worthy. In a Roman triumphal procession the person worthy of honour was the general at the front of the procession, not the prisoners at the end already condemned to death.

Yet it was what the cross achieved that made Jesus worthy of honour. Here are the saints ransomed from every tribe and language and people and nation. Here is an expression of what the General Thanksgiving knows as the 'redemption of the world by our Lord Jesus Christ'.

On Good Friday in Durham Cathedral a wooden cross is brought out to the front of the church and people are invited to come forward and venerate it. Time was when I would have found my Protestant hackles twitching at such an invitation, but now I find it very moving to respond, to come forward and bow the knee before the cross of Christ. For he is worthy of all honour and glory. I look forward in the new creation to bowing the knee and lifting my eyes to my crucified and glorified Lord.

Taking ourselves out of the centre

But if God is worthy of honour and glory – in creation and in the cross (to name just two reasons) – what does offering this praise mean for us and others? Three implications may be suggested. First, giving God the honour and glory takes us out of the centre of the story.

As I have written elsewhere,[3] everything about social media culture says, 'Look at me', but the world was never meant to be mainly about us. Yes, the General Thanksgiving invites us to thank God for the blessings we as individuals have received – both generally in creation and specifically in Christ – but the final

---

3 Philip Plyming, *Being Real: The Apostle Paul's Hardship Narratives and The Stories We Tell Today*, London: SCM Press.

part of the prayer reminds us that the ultimate focus is elsewhere, on the one who is worthy of all praise.

If I turn my eyes left from Bishop Hatfield's tomb, I can gaze upon the Rose Window, one of the glories of Durham Cathedral. It is a depiction in stained glass of part of the scene from Revelation 4 and 5. The 24 elders are there, recognizable through their harps. And in the centre is Jesus Christ. The one around whom everything else radiates. It is he who invites our attention and he who deserves our praise.

I have worked with some extraordinarily gifted colleagues over the years and what has impressed me most is their desire to get out of the way and help people to see Christ and encounter God. Because we are not there to take centre stage. That place is for Jesus alone.

Taking others out of the centre

Second, giving God the honour and glory takes others out of the centre of the story.

I mentioned earlier that the praise ascribed in Revelation 4 and 5 to a crucified Lord was even more extraordinary in its Roman context, but that is not where the political challenge stops. For in focusing on the worthiness of God for ultimate praise and worship, the writer was challenging the Roman political status quo in which Caesar, the Emperor, was the one who called for such loyalty and glory. There is some doubt whether the Emperor Domitian, during whose reign Revelation was probably composed, called himself Master and God, but that is not really the point. As emperor, seated on his throne, he presented himself as the one with ultimate power who deserved absolute loyalty.

It is tempting to think that little has changed. For while rulers and those in authority are not usually so crass as to call themselves gods, some still behave as if they have ultimate control and deserve unquestioning loyalty. Whether it was Hitler, Stalin or Pol Pot in the recent past, or some of the populist leaders on the world stage today, the temptation to let power go to your head seems very strong. Some present themselves as saviours, if not of the world, then certainly their corner of it. I sometimes want to say that the job of saviour has already been taken.

Back to the Rose Window, and if you look carefully at the picture of Jesus in the centre, you can see that he is holding something. It is an orb, similar to the one used by King Charles at his coronation in Westminster Abbey in 2023. The sphere represents the world and atop it is a cross, symbolizing that the world, and all power within it, sits under the authority of Jesus Christ.

I have had the privilege of visiting a number of Orthodox churches over the years, and one of the aspects I most treasure is the picture of Christ either in the apse at the end of the church or in the dome above the centre of the church. Often it is a depiction of Christ Pantocrator – that is, Christ the creator of all things. It usually shows Jesus seated on a throne in glory, as the one through whom all things were made and by whom all things will be judged. Especially when seen from below, it is a powerful reminder that no one – but no one – deserves the central place of honour, besides Christ alone.

World without end

Third, giving God the honour and glory reminds us that we are part of a bigger story.

I remember Professor Andrew Louth making exactly this point when he lectured me on Modern Orthodox Theology here in Durham over 30 years ago. Louth talked of two arches within the story of God and the world.[4] The greater arch stretches between creation and new creation, from the cosmos that God made to the cosmos so transformed that it is both with God and like God (the technical term for this is theosis). Within that greater arch is a smaller arch stretching from sin to salvation, that is, the fall of humankind to redemption won through Jesus Christ. Louth

---

[4] See Andrew Louth, 2007, 'The place of theosis in orthodox theology' in Michael J. Christensen and Jeffrey A. Wittung (eds), *Partakers of the Divine Nature: The History and Development of Deification in the Christian Traditions*, Madison, NJ: Fairleigh Dickinson University Press, p. 35.

argued that in the West we have focused on the smaller arch to the detriment of the greater arch. We have celebrated redemption but forgotten the bigger picture.

The General Thanksgiving suggests that Louth's criticisms might not be entirely justified. For we have seen that Reynolds had both a broad understanding of redemption ('redemption of the world') and also a strong sense of what the hope is that lies before us. And even ending the prayer in the way he does is an invitation to look forward to that time when our place in the bigger story becomes clear, when our place in the new creation sees us transformed from glory into glory. As Charles Wesley put it in his hymn 'Love divine, all loves excelling':

> Finish then thy new creation
> Pure and spotless let us be
> Let us see thy great salvation
> Perfectly restored in thee.
>
> Changed from glory into glory
> Til in heaven we take our place
> Til we cast our crowns before thee
> Lost in wonder, love and praise.

Amen, amen, amen

And so the prayer comes to an end. Rightly so, it started with God and it ended with God. Just as we saw that 'Almighty God, Father of all mercies' was not just an opening formula but an invitation to consider carefully the character of the God to whom we are praying, so we have seen that the final phrase should not be taken as a standard liturgical coda but rather as confirmation of a fundamental reorientation about who the prayer – and the life from which it flows and which it feeds – is all about.

It's not all about us. The prayer is an invitation to thank God for all we have received, but we are to do so not as grateful consumers but rather as participants in the work and life of God himself. In giving thanks we are invited not to voice an elegantly phrased thank you letter but rather to be in relationship with the one from whom all good gifts come and with whom we are eternally bound in love.

We are thus invited to come near the throne of grace (Heb. 4.16) with thanksgiving in our hearts, on our lips and through our lives. We honour the Father from whose creative power all good gifts come. We honour the Son through whose death redemption for the world was secured. We honour the Spirit by whom God's love is poured into our hearts through the means of grace.

This is the invitation offered by Edwards Reynolds and his General Thanksgiving, a prayer that only scraped into the Book of Common Prayer but which has been rightly treasured ever since. Yet if we have explored over the last nine chapters what the different aspects of the prayer mean, we now need to ask how we might take it into our own lives and walk with the Lord. Why might we want to learn it off by heart? When might we want to say it? And what difference might it make when we pray it?

In other words, what next?

Conclusion – Praying the General Thanksgiving Today

I started this book with a story about children and thank you letters, so let's finish by returning to this younger generation.

One of the research streams around gratitude is called the Raising Grateful Children project, which explores gratitude experiences with families as their children grow up. It has identified gratitude as having four components:[1]

- What we *notice* about what we have received – this involves giving attention to small things as well as large.
- How we *think* about why we have been given these things – this involves assessing whether a gift was unmerited or spontaneous, for example.
- How we *feel* about what we have received – this involves tracking our emotions of pleasure or happiness.
- What we *do* in response – this involves either expressing our thanks to the giver or 'paying it forward', that is, giving to others so that they can have a similar experience.

To my mind these components are true for adults as well as children. And we have seen that the General Thanksgiving assists us in all four parts of the journey of giving thanks today.

---

1 Maryam Abdullah et al., 2020, 'How gratitude develops in us' in Jeremy Adam Smith, Kira M. Newman, Jason Marsh and Dacher Keltner (eds), *The Gratitude Project: How the Science of Thankfulness Can Rewire our Brains for Resilience, Optimism and the Greater Good*, Oakland, CA: New Harbinger Publications, pp. 24–5.

First, the prayer invites us to pay attention to what we have received. The words 'creation, preservation and all the blessings of this life' create the opportunity for us to stop and think about the daily blessings we experience which might otherwise pass us by.

Second, the prayer helps us think and reflect about the gift-nature of these blessings. With the focus on God's loving-kindness rather than our own effort, we are encouraged to see these blessings not as rewards we have earned but unmerited gifts we have received.

Third, the prayer touches our emotions about what we have received. This is not a prayer that tots up blessings on an Excel spreadsheet and spits out a bill at the end. Rather, it invites us to offer 'humble and hearty thanks' and prays that our 'hearts will be unfeignedly thankful'. In short, we are to feel the blessings.

Finally, it offers a framework for what we do in response. It is about our lips and our lives, about saying thank you and offering ourselves in the service of God.

Deeper thanks

To this extent, then, the General Thanksgiving models today's good practice in giving thanks. It may be over 350 years old, but in terms of a contemporary understanding of gratitude it is bang up to date.

There are, however, three significant ways in which the General Thanksgiving goes much further than the secular culture of gratitude and invites us to go much deeper in our giving thanks.

First, it invites us into a relationship with the Giver. The General Thanksgiving is not a private gratitude journal entry or a carefully crafted thank you note that we put in the post, hoping that it is received and read. It is a prayer, in which we address and talk to the God who, as James says, 'gives to all generously and ungrudgingly' (James 1.5). We are not thanking into thin air or expressing gratitude to the universe or an unknown deity. We are speaking out our thanks to the 'Father of all mercies', recognizing that 'Every generous act of giving, with every perfect gift,

CONCLUSION

is from above, coming down from the Father of lights' (James 1.17). And as we say this prayer to God, not just once but time after time, we can trust and know that God hears us, that God delights in us, that God is pleased when we turn our hearts in thanksgiving to him.

Let me ask: is this our picture of God? Or do we see God the way the elder son saw his father in the Parable of the Two Sons (Luke 15.11–32)? He thought everything had to be earned and nothing would be given. And so he feared judgement rather than received love. Or do we pray as the General Thanksgiving invites us to, that is, to a God who is the Father of all mercies, who gives good gifts, who does not need but who treasures our words of thanks and praise?

Second, the General Thanksgiving highlights enduring reasons for giving thanks. As we have seen, the heart of the prayer is a meditation on God's inestimable love – poured out in the past as Christ offered his life for the redemption of the world, poured out in the present through the means of grace by which we know God with us, and poured out in the future as we hold on to the hope of glory. This is the reminder we all need: that while it is good and right that we give thanks for the blessings of this life, that which we receive every day, beneath all these are the lasting and enduring reasons to give thanks for God, reasons that are true every day whatever is going on in our lives.

If we see Jesus not simply as a human being but as the one who died to redeem the world, if we see the Bible, prayer and Holy Communion not simply as human creations but as ways we can encounter and receive Christ today, if we see our hope of glory not as optimistic wishful thinking but part of God's certain future, then we have solid reasons for gratitude that go far beyond what this week is going to bring. Fundamentally, our giving thanks need not be shaken by whether our world is looking great or grim; the chief reasons to give thanks are not dependent on events or emotions – they are true every morning.

I wonder, are we being invited to see afresh this heart of gratitude? Perhaps there is one of the three aspects of God's inestimable love – past, present and future – that we are being called to be attentive to?

Third, the General Thanksgiving offers resources for our response. We have seen that the response described in the prayer is a whole-life response, one that involves our lips and our lives as we pursue holiness and righteousness. To this extent, therefore, it is a decision that we make, namely to offer all that we have in the service of Christ, and this decision is one that we are invited to revisit on a daily basis as we live lives of thankfulness.

But here's the exciting bit: we are not doing this on our own. The General Thanksgiving is not simply a prayer of giving thanks but also a prayer that asks God to help us give thanks. We slightly glossed over the phrase 'we beseech thee' at the start of the second half of the prayer but it is actually crucial. Because it is a request that God will so work in our hearts that we will be filled with thanksgiving, so that our offering of ourselves springs not out of duty but out of genuine thanks.

In other words, the resources for giving thanks do not lie in ourselves. Whether we think of ourselves as grateful people or not (and the evidence for gratitude as a trait is mixed) we can all ask God to help us give thanks. When our own capacity to give thanks is at a low ebb, perhaps because of tough things we are living through or have lived through, this prayer can help us.

Praying the General Thanksgiving

Above all, the General Thanksgiving is a prayer not to be studied but to be prayed. The aim of this book has not been to help us know more about the General Thanksgiving but rather to help us use it in our prayer lives. What might that look like?

The first step I want to suggest is to encourage you to memorize the prayer – that is, learn it off by heart. As I said in the Introduction, this is what generations of people did as part of their confirmation classes, with the result that they could recall it well over 60 years later. The General Thanksgiving was a prayer that accompanied them through good times and bad. When you have memorized a prayer it means at least two things: first, you can pray it whenever and wherever – you are dependent neither on a book nor on how spiritual you are feeling. Second, a mem-

CONCLUSION

orized prayer enters your spiritual bloodstream. The more you say it, not just by rote but carefully and thoughtfully, the more it shapes you. In other words, praying the General Thanksgiving makes you more thankful.

Now I know what you may be thinking as I mention learning the prayer off by heart: 'That sounds really scary.' And it is true that more recent generations are used to having all information on their phones, so memorizing things isn't as necessary. But I think we all have a good chance of memorizing the prayer if we follow a few simple tips:

- Learn it one phrase at a time. In other words, don't try and learn the whole thing but just the first phrase. 'Almighty God and Father of all mercies, we thine unworthy servants' is enough to start with. Then add the next phrase to that one and say them both. And add one phrase at a time until you can remember the whole prayer.
- Learn it by saying it out loud. We learn things better when we use our bodies (i.e. our mouths and our ears). It can feel odd but it will make the experience so much easier.
- If you find it easier to learn the contemporary version of the prayer in the Appendix, please use that one.
- Once you have learned it, pray it once a day until it becomes second nature.

Then the question is when you pray it. There is, of course, no right time, but I have found it helpful to use it first thing in the morning to orientate me for the day ahead. This is particularly the case when I have not slept well and am anxious about the day to come. The prayer helps me approach the day in a thankful and not a fearful spirit.

Another good time I have found is after receiving Holy Communion. As we saw in Chapter 5, Holy Communion is one of the means of grace, and it focuses us on God's inestimable love past, present and future. But Holy Communion is also about our response, and as I have prayed after receiving the sacrament, I have found the General Thanksgiving helps me express what I want to offer back to God.

Lastly, it is a good prayer to pray with others. Originally, of course, it was designed for use in church (although over time the Book of Common Prayer became a personal devotional book) and so would have been said either by the minister on behalf of others or actually by the whole congregation together. So it would make total sense to use it in a church service, perhaps at the end of the intercessions, or in a home group or study group. If you are using this book as part of a Lent Course, you may want to end each session by praying it together.

How to pray it? You can of course just pray it straight through as you might say any prayer, but I have found it helpful on occasions to pause after each phrase and think about its meaning. Taking time to reflect on the Lord's goodness and loving-kindness, on the means of grace, on my own call to holiness and righteousness, helps the prayer connect with my own heart and life.

A helpful prayer

To finish with, let me suggest four ways in which, as we pray it, the General Thanksgiving can help us in our walk with the Lord.

First, the prayer can help us notice reasons to give thanks. The phrase 'all the blessings of this life' is wonderfully inclusive and invites us to give attention to the blessings that can so easily pass us by. A nutritious soup for lunch. Bright daffodils on the edge of the road. A text from a friend checking on how I am doing. These are all reasons to give thanks to God, and the General Thanksgiving invites me to pause, to notice and to praise God. Whether we write them in a journal or not (and I think that depends on the type of person we are) we are still invited to capture and pause with daily reasons to give thanks.

Second, the prayer can prompt us to thank others. If we are regularly thanking God in the framework offered by the General Thanksgiving, I think one of the results will be that our hearts become more thankful and we express those thanks to others. In other words, our disposition to give thanks will be nurtured and so we will be motivated to express our gratitude to others.

CONCLUSION

As I recognize my dependence on God for all I have received, so I also acknowledge my dependence on others through whom God works. I am thankful to God for the calling to serve as Dean of Durham, but I am also so thankful to God for my colleagues who serve with me. And so I thank them, not to curry favour with them but because having thanked God for them it seems only right to thank them too.

Third, the prayer can help us to be content. We discussed in the Introduction how some people are suspicious of gratitude culture because it can be seen as neglecting inequality or social injustice. We also saw how it can be weaponized to reinforce feelings of subservience. The General Thanksgiving is not to be used in that way, not least because the call to righteousness in the prayer is a commitment to seek justice in all its forms. Furthermore, we should never require someone to pray the General Thanksgiving as a way of silencing their concerns or reinforcing a sense of dependence.

However, the General Thanksgiving can be helpful in inviting us to step off the materialistic travelator that says we always need more. When human beings are described as 'consumers', it is an expression of a culture that is premised on our not being satisfied with our lot. Now that served us well as we sought to lift people out of poverty and create a better standard of living for all, but in the twenty-first-century West this has created a lust for more things that fails to recognize what we already have.

This is how researchers Dacher Keltner and Jason Marsh put it: 'One of the traps of materialism … is that it locates sources of happiness in shiny new things. Indeed, research suggests that materialistic people have unrealistically high expectations for the amount of happiness material goods will bring them.'[2] By contrast, giving thanks 'helps us savour the good in our lives rather than take it for granted while yearning for what's next'.[3]

The Apostle Paul, writing from prison to the church in Philippi, knew what it was to have lots and to have little, and had taken this lesson from his experience: 'I have learned to be content with

---

2 Dacher Keltner and Jason Marsh, 'Can gratitude beat materialism?', *The Gratitude Project*, p. 182.

3 Keltner and Marsh, 'Can gratitude beat materialism?', p. 183.

whatever I have' (Phil. 4.11). By focusing on enduring reasons for gratitude, the General Thanksgiving does not mean we stop working hard, but it allows us to be grateful for what we already have rather than resentful of what we don't have.

Fourth, the prayer can help us to keep going. We noted earlier that these are demanding times to live in – both in the world and in the Church – let alone what any one of us is having to face in our personal lives. For myself, I find the experience of being a survivor of church-based child sexual abuse increasingly challenging as the Church of England as an institution frequently struggles to put survivors at the heart of its response. I find trauma responses catching me unawares and leading to really intense emotions.

Whatever our challenges – from without or within – one of the impacts it can have on us is a feeling of disorientation, of sensing that there are few fixed points and that everything is uncertain. In that space it can feel tempting to give up or step back from the Christian walk and the roles we have been called to.

In those times, the General Thanksgiving is not the only prayer we are invited to pray. We are invited, for example, as I have written elsewhere, to be real about our struggles in the belief that God can meet us in the most unlikely places.[4] But the General Thanksgiving offers us the chance to reorientate ourselves around the mercies of God, the blessings of life in Christ, and the heart of what we are called to be and do. It is one of the reasons why I think learning it off by heart is so good: when we are disorientated it is hard to find the words to pray, but Edward Reynolds has given us words to help us.

Giving thanks in all circumstances

Paul exhorted the Christians in Thessaloniki to 'give thanks in all circumstances' (1 Thess. 5.18). The General Thanksgiving helps us to do just that. It provides a framework that is both attentive to our daily lives but also connects with a bigger picture of

---

4 Philip Plyming, 2023, *Being Real: The Apostle Paul's Hardship Narratives and The Stories We Tell Today*, London: SCM Press.

CONCLUSION

God's love and invites us to make a whole-life response, so that our Christian discipleship is not about earning God's favour but responding to God's inestimable love. If we pray the prayer carefully and thoughtfully we will find ourselves giving thanks not *for* all circumstances but *in* all circumstances, and our hearts will be changed as a result.

Bishop Edward Reynolds wrote the General Thanksgiving at a time of personal trial, ecclesial turmoil and political upheaval. Sneaking into the 1662 edition of the Book of Common Prayer at the last minute, it has taken its place as one of the best-loved and most-used of all the prayers. Within a culture where it is increasingly recognized that gratitude is good for us, the General Thanksgiving helps us to take that giving thanks to a deeper level, one that is rooted in the unchanging loving-kindness of God. It is a gift for today's Church and for every follower of Jesus Christ. I pray it is a blessing for you now and in the years to come.

Appendix

A Contemporary Form of the General Thanksgiving

Almighty God, Father of all mercies,
we your unworthy servants give you most humble and
    hearty thanks
for all your goodness and loving kindness.
We bless you for our creation, preservation,
and all the blessings of this life;
but above all for your immeasurable love
in the redemption of the world by our Lord Jesus Christ,
for the means of grace, and for the hope of glory.
And give us, we pray, such a sense of all your mercies
that our hearts may be thankful,
and that we show forth your praise, not only with our lips,
    but in our lives,
by giving up ourselves to your service,
and by walking before you in holiness and righteousness
    all our days;
through Jesus Christ our Lord,
to whom, with you and the Holy Spirit,
be all honour and glory, for ever and ever.
Amen.[1]

---

[1] *New Patterns for Worship*, 2002, London: Church House Publishing, p. 236.

Bibliography

Abdullah, Maryam, Giacomo Bono, Jeffrey Froh, Andrea Hussong, and Kira Newman, 2020, 'How gratitude develops in us' in Jeremy Adam Smith, Kira M. Newman, Jason Marsh and Dacher Keltner (eds), *The Gratitude Project: How the Science of Thankfulness Can Rewire our Brains for Resilience, Optimism and the Greater Good*, Oakland, CA: New Harbinger Publications.

Adam Smith, Jeremy, 2020, 'How to cultivate gratitude in yourself' in Jeremy Adam Smith, Kira M. Newman, Jason Marsh and Dacher Keltner (eds), *The Gratitude Project: How the Science of Thankfulness Can Rewire our Brains for Resilience, Optimism and the Greater Good*, Oakland, CA: New Harbinger Publications.

Barrington-Ward, Simon, 2007, *The Jesus Prayer*, Oxford: The Bible Reading Fellowship.

Church of England, 2000, *Common Worship: Services and Prayers for the Church of England*, London: Church House Publishing.

Church of England, 2002, *New Patterns for Worship*, London: Church House Publishing.

Cuming, G. J., 1983, *The Godly Order: Texts and Studies Relating to the Book of Common Prayer*, London: Alcuin Club.

Emmons, Robert, and Jeremy Adam Smith, 2020, 'What gratitude is and why it matters' in Jeremy Adam Smith, Kira M. Newman, Jason Marsh and Dacher Keltner (eds), *The Gratitude Project: How the Science of Thankfulness Can Rewire our Brains for Resilience, Optimism and the Greater Good*, Oakland, CA: New Harbinger Publications.

Hatchett, Marion J., 1995, *Commentary on the American Prayer Book*, San Francisco, CA: HarperCollins.

Hitz, Zena, 2023, *A Philosopher Looks at the Religious Life*, Cambridge: Cambridge University Press.

Hugo, Victor, 1980, *Les Misérables*, translated by Norman Denny, London: Penguin Books.

Keay, Anna, 2023, *The Restless Republic: Britain without a Crown*, London: HarperCollins.

Keltner, Dacher, and Jason Marsh, 2020, 'Can gratitude beat materialism?' in Jeremy Adam Smith, Kira M. Newman, Jason Marsh and Dacher Keltner (eds), *The Gratitude Project: How the Science of*

Thankfulness Can Rewire our Brains for Resilience, Optimism and the Greater Good, Oakland, CA: New Harbinger Publications.

Lewis, C. S., 1942, *The Weight of Glory*, London: SPCK.

Louth, Andrew (ed.), 2017, *The Way of a Pilgrim: Candid Tales of a Wanderer to His Spiritual Father*, London: Penguin Classics.

Louth, Andrew, 2007, 'The place of theosis in orthodox theology' in Michael J. Christensen and Jeffrey A. Wittung (eds), *Partakers of the Divine Nature: The History and Development of Deification in the Christian Traditions*, Madison, NJ: Fairleigh Dickinson University Press.

Methodist Church, 1999, *The Methodist Worship Book*, Peterborough: Methodist Publishing House.

Plyming, Philip, 2023, *Being Real: The Apostle Paul's Hardship Narratives and The Stories We Tell Today*, London: SCM Press.

Roberts, Brian K., 2023, *Building Durham Cathedral*, Cheltenham: The History Press.

Suttie, Jill, 2020, 'Is gratitude the path to a better world?' in Jeremy Adam Smith, Kira M. Newman, Jason Marsh and Dacher Keltner (eds), *The Gratitude Project: How the Science of Thankfulness Can Rewire our Brains for Resilience, Optimism and the Greater Good*, Oakland, CA: New Harbinger Publications.

Tozer, A. W., 1984, *The Knowledge of the Holy: The Attributes of God, Their Meaning in the Christian Life*, Bromley: STL.

Ward, Benedicta, 1992, *The Spirituality of Saint Cuthbert*, Oxford: Fairacres Publications.

Webb, Simon (ed.), 2016, *Bede's Life of St Cuthbert*, Durham: Langley Press.

Westminster Assembly (1643–52), 1646, *The Humble Advice of the Assembly of Divines, Now by Authority of Parliament Sitting at Westminster, Concerning Part of a Confession of Faith Presented by them Lately to both Houses of Parliament*, London: Printed for the Company of Stationers.

Wong, Joel, Joshua Brown, Christina Armenta, Sonja Lyubomirsky, Summer Allen, Amie Gordon and Kira Newman, 2020, 'Why gratitude is good for us' in Jeremy Adam Smith, Kira M. Newman, Jason Marsh and Dacher Keltner (eds), *The Gratitude Project: How the Science of Thankfulness Can Rewire our Brains for Resilience, Optimism and the Greater Good*, Oakland, CA: New Harbinger Publications.

Wright, N. T., 1994, *Following Jesus: Biblical Reflections on Discipleship*, London: SPCK.

Wyatt, John, 2009, *Matters of Life and Death*, revised edition, Nottingham: IVP.

www.ingramcontent.com/pod-product-compliance
Lightning Source LLC
Chambersburg PA
CBHW020539080526
44583CB00013B/917